WADE PIERSON

SOULPUNK

a tale of time in poetry

First published by Wade Pierson 2025

Copyright © 2025 by Wade Pierson

All rights reserved. No part of this publication may be reproduced, stored or transmitted in any form or by any means, electronic, mechanical, photocopying, recording, scanning, or otherwise without written permission from the publisher. It is illegal to copy this book, post it to a website, or distribute it by any other means without permission.

Wade Pierson asserts the moral right to be identified as the author of this work.

Designations used by companies to distinguish their products are often claimed as trademarks. All brand names and product names used in this book and on its cover are trade names, service marks, trademarks and registered trademarks of their respective owners. The publishers and the book are not associated with any product or vendor mentioned in this book. None of the companies referenced within the book have endorsed the book.

First edition

ISBN: 979-8-218-87313-4

This book was professionally typeset on Reedsy. Find out more at reedsy.com

To Mom, Dad, Jasmine, and Shane

Contents

Preface	v
The Question	1
SOULPUNK: PART ONE	2
Oblivion	3
Crabs Inna Barrel	5
Waist Deep	7
There's A Pot Boiling	9
Stillness	14
Bonjour Raven	15
The Duality of Testosterone in A Rapper's Boyhood	18
Love Through The Revolutions of The Sun	22
It's The Reason Why	23
Memory	25
The Thing	26
And She Was Already Lonely	28
Many Rocks, Many Hard Places	30
Letter To Grandma	31
21	32
Mother	34
Maybe	36
Smile In The Garden	37
Geronimo	39
Of Course	42
Stagnant Heart	44

Fracturée	45
Pink	47
And All That She Showed Me In 24 Hours	48
Tethered Lust	49
Down The Road	51
Symphony of Doubt	53
Fold Your Hands, My Son	57
What I'd Do For Friends	58
Ça va, Raven?	60
The Time Keeps Passing	63
The Corners of My Mouth Shall Rise	65
Holster	67
Scrape	68
Oh Brother, Where Is Our God?	71
Dreadful Sighs	74
No Crutch For Love	75
Spares	77
Sand	79
I Should Let You Go, But…	88
Still Both of Yours	89
Requiem For A Bluebird	91
War	96
And I Avoided The Song She Might've Sung	101
A Quiet Harm	103
Blood Betrayal	104
My Cousin Named Cultural Stigma	109
Brothers In Spring(time)	110
A Reflection	121
Talk To Me (About Your World)	123
God, Won't You End Me	133
The Winds of Mankind	134

Grief Waters	135
The Great Brown Heron & The Bronze Woman	143
SOULPUNK: PART TWO	157
Bone Man In The Rays	158
Fear & Valor (A Letter)	161
Breathe	163
1940	165
If I Knew The Words Back Then	168
Senses	174
Ten Years To Send You On Your Way	176
Au Revoir Raven	177
And She Whispered To Me "It's Okay To Live"	182
Dognation	184
November 5th, 2024	185
Same Divine Word	187
To Whom The Light Touches	189
A Divided House Will Fall	191
Diner (Table For 1 Broke Man)	194
Black American Ambiance	198
Bags Packed	200
By The Curb	202
Sandcastles	205
The People's Cocktail	206
What's New, Friends?	208
Reconciliation	211
Man Standing	212
Finding Father (A Letter)	213
Angels For Jasmine (A Letter)	220
You've Got Mail	222
Peace	223
Sky High Loves	226

No Name	229
Words For A Sweet Lady	230
Dear Juliet	236
Son	238
I Hear You	240
Letter To Shane	248
Your Uncle's Words	255
Kinder Man	257
What's Your Name?	259
All That I Carry	261
Remain	262
You Snuck Into God's Office?	265
The Man Upstairs	268
Soulpunk	289
About the Author	292

Preface

Hi,

To begin with, I must say that this book is a poetic memoir, not a self-help book. There isn't much for me to say other than that, but a few things below.

1- Everything is in the poetry, letters, and essays I've written for myself, for you, and for God. I grew up on the East Coast for half of my life. The other half, for the most part, has been spent in California thus far. This book is split into two parts: the first half revolves around whether I wanted to live or not. The second half is choosing to live.

2- Originally, "SOULPUNK" was a screenplay of mine in progress about a man in a cyberpunk world questioning if he was human or a machine. If he had a soul or not. Back then, the book's title was "The Great Brown Heron & The Bronze Woman", the poem at the climax of this book. Suddenly, I found myself thinking, the summer before I announced the book to the public, "Man, 'Soulpunk' sounds so hardcore."

3- I am a work in progress, not to be perfect, but to become more human. To identify in others what I've identified in myself throughout time, and to do, at the very least, whatever I can to help them not only remain alive, but live. And to those I do not know or who are no longer in my life, I hope you take away at least one word from this book: love.
   -Wade P.

The Question

Live^1 /liv/ - verb
   1. Remain alive.
   - Be alive at a specified time.
   - Spend one's life in a particular way or under particular circumstances.
   - Supply oneself with the means of subsistence.
   - Survive in someone's mind; be remembered.
   - Have an exciting or fulfilling life.
   2. Make one's home in a particular place or with a particular person.

Slapped on the back
   pulled from the womb of our many mothers
   we've found ourselves with the breath of life
   and so the question remains…

"how do you live?"

SOULPUNK: PART ONE

the words i say
reveal my face
look at me
am i a liar?
can you tell?

i told you to look
but you need listen
i am a lover
no matter the lies i tell

Oblivion

life
   surrounding me by a mist
   a thick darkness that covers my face
   lonely
   as it is always
   fore i lay - thinking of you

i wonder
   if you lay thinking of me
   am i worth your hours
   as you are worth mine?
   or should i lie here
   unmoved by you
   in the depths of my oblivion?

for years, he has been lost
   and i have searched for him
   fore i cannot find him
   but i know him
   i am him -
   i am the man in the mirror
   but i am far from home.

i know you, but i cannot remember your voice
   we've met before, but i cannot remember where
   these thoughts...
   your thoughts, feel real
   and i know it is just the mist
   clouding my mind and memory
   a blockade of darkness
   but i am often reminded it is more than simple thoughts
   it feels like my past,
   but is that possible?

the things i yell about, she won't
   the things i dream about, she doesn't

i wake
   standing before the mirror,
   not remembering
   not knowing...
   who you are,
   or why i am awake.

Crabs Inna Barrel

late night
   grandmas front porch
   some older black man arrived
   was it grandmas boyfriend
   can i just say granddad?
   or was it one of his friends?
   someone dropped off a bucket
   scratch noises scared me that late
   i was at least younger than eight
   someone lifted the lid
   too many crabs to count before i got worried.

someone picked up the barrel
   brought it into the kitchen
   wooden tiles that seeped when you stood upon 'em
   grandma wasted no time
   she never did waste time in the kitchen
   weren't too long before we were all outside.

grandmas big backyard
   plastic white table
   plastic white chairs

move too much 'n one of the legs'll snap
eating crabs
legs and arms snapped
barely the ones i had though
hands too small
biceps too small
not strong enough to get all the shell off
i had a bigger crunch than y'all.

tore up mosquito bitten legs
   fireflies in the bushes
   fireflies above us
   remember laughter
   butter drenched cheeks and fingers
   was this before or after the tomato seeds were planted?
   before or after mom got into that car accident?
   the first time i ever felt anxiety
   and in the same night
   relief when she walked up to the door.

can't remember when any of it happened
   but i remember
   you both were older than me
   you may remember differently than me
   but i sure do remember
   a good time behind grandmas house
   ever so gently.

Waist Deep

at thirteen, i found you in the rain
   our bodies were soaked
   you were ready to sink in

depressed - your scars stayed covered up
   no one questioned all your long sleeves
   hair down, waist deep in the lake

distressed - you gave all my gifts up
   said your last goodbye to me
   i couldn't leave your side

i begged you to stop
   was it tears or the rain
   that made you come out of the lake?

too cold - i warmed your body up
   maybe the water woke you up, but
   i'll walk you home to your ma

too cold - but brighter days are comin' up
   smiled after like we unified

SOULPUNK

you got home alive

There's A Pot Boiling

there's a pot boiling
   moms spaghetti
   grandmas recipe
   maybe
   grass stained jeans
   in the knees of course
   army dodge ball slides
   or acorn fights
   or besting everyone
   in hide and seek

pool at the boys and girls club
   one on one match with joseph
   i actually beat him
   even though he had
   what?
   nine years on me
   don't know if you remember that
   jasmine
   or if you remember that
   shane

remember the rentals dad used to pull up in?
  sitting in front of the heater when it snowed
  socks for gloves
  playin' taps on curbs with other kids
  jamming the mattress
  between the walls of the stairwell
  and insanely sliding down it
  new york trips and moms house parties
  thanksgiving in yonkers or brooklyn?
  or somewhere else in the big apple?
  had red velvet for the first time
  or the first time i remember
  or that one time
  the three of us were gonna fight
  those bad ass kids in grandma's neighborhood
  or the stupid time
  we got caught trying to sneak the kittens home
  in a backpack in the back of mom's car?
  or sleep overs at grandma's green house
  is that why green's your favorite color
  brother?
  wonder if it became mine
  because of you

  bombing the hill in meade village
    on bikes
    broken brakes
    i didn't wear shoes half the time
    i'd brake with my feet
    riding home with holes in my socks
    with a bike you'd stolen

THERE'S A POT BOILING

    or going down on scooters
    careful how we spun that thing
    might take an ankle or two out

i remember i was scared to ride on the back of your pedals
    jasmine had no problem
    but i think there was a time when you flipped
    i'd watch on from the curb
    i wanted to
    but i never held your shoulders

i remember wearing the clothes you grew out of
    i never asked
    i'd just find them and wear 'em in secret
    as if donning a costume
    trying to become cool
    look cool
    be
    like
    you

remember how we used to sing and dance
    or just goof around
    in the mirror maybe
    but always in your room
    jasmine
    i know we used to do whatever
    in front of your laptop camera
    the one dad got you
    memorizing song verses
    you be this part

i'll be that part
he'll be that part
dear sister
your voice could rip through a black cloud
and save anyone
even God Himself
should He ever need saving
and if there was anyone brave enough
to pull His hand after you destroyed the gates of hell
it'd be you
dear brother

there are no warnings
   of bad possibilities
   when life presents good enough distractions
   or when you're just too far away to see the signs

someone in the family
   or something in the family
   keeps telling us
   there's a pot boiling
   watch the water
   or it'll fall over the top

but we come from a strong tree
   of strength
   of beauty
   of health ignorance
   of hidden pains and secrets

oh how many i've discovered

THERE'S A POT BOILING

just by listening to everyone
or reading everything

or by seeing how everyone reacted
when we realized
the tree was losing it's memory

Stillness

18 homes in 25 years
were they all homes?
i never quite knew stillness...
only in prayer.

Bonjour Raven

i know the great road of pain
   life makes one undertake
   to write such profound truth
   though i am only fifteen
   i unfortunately know that name

my messy
   ragged papers
   stained yellow
   holding onto old words
   phrases and dreams that once saved my life
   ones i created
   ones i found
   before and after
   leaving God in the night
   and coming back to Him
   when the time was right

i took up track
   to run for something
   i took up journalism
   to write for something

SOULPUNK

    i took up french
    to speak for something

yet, i still don't know how to go as deep as you
    i feel as if my lines are blurred
    reality and fiction take over me together
    there's only a consistent safe haven in the latter

i don't know the last time my heart neared exploding
    maybe it was six months ago when i met you
    the same acne still lives on my face today
    as i reckon with the fact i may never see you again

something about the two of us
    two teenage poets trauma bonding
    i guess i am a bit of a dramatic person
    after all, i did start theatre this year

i don't know what to do with some of our memories
    the gentle wetness of your tears on my shoulder
    as i played you a song i saved for my own sorrows
    sitting side by side in gym class

or our roughly made san francisco plans
    turning an abandoned warehouse into a studio
    making a mixtape together and saving tons of money
    in case we get ripped off by a record company

i sent you something i'd written
    after i found out you were to be home schooled
    and you told me

BONJOUR RAVEN

"poetry is a lost art, but you definitely found it"

but, my dear raven,
    how will i make it through high school
    if, in these long and foreign hallways,
    i can no longer find you?

The Duality of Testosterone in A Rapper's Boyhood

don't hit my phone like you used to
   ignoring you, i am not used to
   but we better off just not talkin'
   we better off if i don't reply

growin' from this is a curse and blessin'
   first nigga to ever have your parents blessin'
   and for some time now we on our separate ways
   but these new women got me second guessin'

that's been an issue
   that's always pressin' on my mind 'n shit
   she talkin' 'bout threesomes on my line n' shit
   she talkin' 'bout raw on some temptin' shit
   like she don't know
   what
   a damn rubber is
   i hold
   my head
   ain't got
   no rubber

THE DUALITY OF TESTOSTERONE IN A RAPPER'S BOYHOOD

shit

ain't got no rubber
   shit...

but fuck it i don't care
   but maybe i should
   girl we should
   "what?"

stop fuckin' around

'cause i could get caught up
   look at how a nigga was brought up
   like a bastard
   parents ain't marry after the fact that i was born
   shit, i'm still a lil torn
   but fuck it
   girl, when we fuckin'?
   'cause i'm stupid
   i don't listen to my own conscious
   i'm ignoring all that past shit, past lessons
   gotta focus on the future, gotta lotta questions

oh my when that beat drop
   let that heat bang
   she said "let that seat drop back
   lemme sit on that thang"
   i been thinkin' 'bout when you was finna
   let that p pop
   bussin' down that thang

    i just got a quick nut bust
    ain't really think 'bout it enough, fuck
    ...

clouds in the wind
    you been flyin' in
    grew up in the inner city
    you flew out the lions den
    it's crazy how deep i knew you back then
    but then again

somebody clipped your wings
    you fell in my lap
    wasn't worthy of your love
    you gave me a chance at that

somehow i found paradise in you
    but heaven is right above you
    heaven is right above us
    look at where we met at
    i mean, look at the place we come from

you was a young lady tryin' not to cry
    i was a young nigga trynna add up to some'
    you turned into a young woman that hated goodbyes
    i was a young nigga trynna get some

and now you just a young queen
    and i'm just a young king
    and nowadays we don't talk
    but it's all good

THE DUALITY OF TESTOSTERONE IN A RAPPER'S BOYHOOD

'cause i hope the best for you
and i hope you do the same for me.

Love Through The Revolutions of The Sun

sunrise
it is too early to ask for her love
maybe
if i give a gentle whisper
she'll come around...
in due time.

...

sunset
she tucks in her love
i have had it all this time
but me and all my imperfections
do not know how to return the favor...
yet, by tomorrow, i will have learned something.

It's The Reason Why

from your sight
  i'd wag my tail
  if i had one

from your scent
  i'd take a bite
  just a playful one

from your voice
  i'd bark in joy
  hope it don't scare none

you stir my senses
  drive me mad
  'cause i love you

you add color
  you add light
  you make me hopeful

tell me breathe
  play some jazz

SOULPUNK

   make it soulful

stir my senses
  make me mad
    it's why i love you

Memory

you asked me if i had talked to your son
   my uncle casper
   but dear grandmother
   i did not have the strength to remind you
   he has been gone for years

would such a lie
   identify
   as a sin
   in God's eyes?

have You no mercy after all this time?

The Thing

i don't understand

this thing
    this dark, impending manifestation
    of doom
    it has followed me across this nation
    from baltimore to california
    and still, i know not where it comes from

only that i find myself yearning for it
    reaching for it
    or is it mirrored
    and it's reaching for me?

is it me?
    if i'm doing it
    then it's doing it
    if it's doing it
    then i'm…

i cannot hold a job
    i cannot hold a relationship

THE THING

    with God or my lady
    not even with reality

maybe this thing was growing all along
    like a mass that can't be stopped
    it can only be ignored for so long
    and when it makes its presence known again
    i know all too well that it is wrong

sleep for now
    you brazen lion
    let me have what little peace
    i can find
    and be offered
    by friend or foe
    lover or hater
    solitude or gathering
    God or unknown

And She Was Already Lonely

and you say you don't mind
   how i get sleep paralysis at night
   waking you up at 3am.

and you say you don't mind
   how i let myself go sometimes
   hair unkempt for years.

and you say you don't mind
   the long showers without you
   hot water that only soothes me.

and you say you don't mind
   how i've had to borrow money
   no intentions of paying it back.

and you say you don't mind
   how little you felt loved today
   holding out hope for tomorrows.

and you say you don't mind
   how selfish i've been lately

AND SHE WAS ALREADY LONELY

   completely oblivious to my own actions.

and you say you don't mind
   how anxious i've been lately
   safekeeping your darkest secrets.

i gave up on us
   because i bit off more than i could chew
   the first time i uttered the words
   i love you.

something unmendable happened inside
   skin unable to feel the touch of another
   like the body has been asleep for far too long
   and so the heart, too,
   has become numb to connection.

i said goodbye first,
   so may God bless you first.

Many Rocks, Many Hard Places

my life is all a circle
living through different jungles
and trynna learn all my lessons
'fore i run outta my adolescence
laughin' in these rap sessions
stories breaking me down
niggas fightin' depression
all i feel is oppression
...
what sailor will throw me overboard?
tell me your prayers and pleas
when the sea calms

i need a Word with God.

Letter To Grandma

dear grandma,

   i never knew my fathers mother, nor his father, nor my mothers father. so i put all of that grandness on you. and your departure from this world has ripped through my soul like a great sword of misery. i see images of myself in a burning pain, but when i open my eyes, nothing falls from them. i want to cry so bad that it feels like i can't breathe, but for some reason i can't find that amount of tears for you. i only shed six or seven the morning of your passing on the phone with your daughter, my mother. maybe no amount of tears can equal the hole inside. maybe the hole keeps my tears trapped. i don't know... i'm curious as to how God plans on filling this massive pit.

how is it up there? is it as beautiful as you? i bet it is. God blessed me with a theatre show that has sixties music in it. wonder if it's because of you.

your grandson,
   sean.

21

sat down with myself and said hey you need to change
   rip out all your roots and start a new way.

maybe you need a drink
   hey
   maybe you need to get laid.

21 for four months and i'm just gettin' drunk
   21 for four months and i'm already in love
   21 for four months and i'm just getting laid off
   21 for four months and i'm already fucked

the girl i fell for had to go back home
   quarantine really has jokes of its own
   my uncle i haven't seen since i was young passed from covid-19
   and now my aunt is fighting it all alone.

21 for four months and i'm just getting old
   21 for four months and i'm just starting to fold
   21 for four months and i'm just getting stoned
   21 for four months and i'm just now realizing i never wanted to be this alone...

21

the world is shutting down,
and i don't recognize this lonely road.

Mother

mother
   i wear this frown
   my first sight was love
   then the world burning down
   and after all the love you poured around
   the world
   is still burning alive

mother
   take back this crown
   i've put in a word with God
   to strike me down
   but He has not answered this prayer now
   dear mother
   i am still alive

i wear the necklace you gave me
   i rub it for good luck and protection
   others seem to work fine, but mine…
   did the power of the cross run out?

three doves sing a song

MOTHER

how could this world turn and still be so wrong?
the amazon river has less salt
than these tears that stretch wide and long

are they running down my face now?

Maybe

maybe we'll make our sad days happy
   our hesitations snappy

winter, summer
   our gentle kisses rougher

goodbye, constant embraces
   flicker, wild blazes

last words, endless conversation
   last fight, humorous flirtation

what a thing we could have
   if we gave it another laugh

Smile In The Garden

well Mary's in my garden
   with a small, baby J
   She smiled and said pardon
   and moved, i did

and i tried to tell you of a sight beautiful
   but your eyes just rolled inside
   and all you said
   was that
   you now reject religion

but this wasn't the Kings book
   it was in the world that we took delight...

i wept
   with the same pain as He
   i was depressed
   but gave you pleasantries

my attempt at affection
   was disregarded inside you

the ground broke to a hole
    and swallowed all my love whole
    so
    i climbed out of your soul.

Geronimo

no role models over here, shit
   ever since i was a kid, shit
     had to learn how to burn my own bridges
     had to learn to get over them old bitches

wonderin'
   which sin is the greatest?
   is it my vanity or greed
   or my fiendin' for the riches?

'cause i'm just a young nigga with a cross around his neck
   had a couple jobs just to get a decent check
   got fucked over by people who had my respect
   that's what happens when
   all you know
   how to do
   is expect

gotta learn how to lower that shit
   can't duck
   that's how you get hit with bullshit
   that's how you end up inna ditch

feelin' like you can't get up
'cause a spell placed on you by a witch

...

depression hittin' real hard
   lost you 'cause i am the way i am
   i don't even know what i feel inside
   guess that makes me a lesser man

karma is a mothafucka - how don't i remember her?
   everything that she put me through on this earth?
   half my childhood – scared we gon' end up in the dirt
   new shelter, new school – i ain't gotta clean shirt
   another shelter, 'nother school – goddammit life hurts

can't find the right one
   all these new bitches flirts
   finally found the right one
   and we couldn't make it work

prolly fucked up 'cause love equals pain for me
   i been searchin' for that since i moved to cali

i been lost on what the word "love" really means
   i been mixin' lust in my drinks
   but i was already crazy
   'cause i'm too far gone when i think
   girl
   you too far gone with the wrong niggas
   shit

GERONIMO

you ain't never asked what i think

guess i'll trade my two cents in for some ink
   'cause lately i been feelin' shit that make a nigga think
   lately i been feelin' shit that put me on the brink…

Of Course

got plans to kick it and have dinner i'll pick you up around five
   you ain't text me back til like nine thirty-five
   a.m.
   bit- i mean girl
   why you playin'?

do i stand anywhere with you?
   if i do it's prolly on one foot
   hoppin' around tellin' you how good you look

look
   nah never mind you still on ya phone
   even when i'm near you it seem like you still out ya zone

now i'm just ramblin'
   gamblin' with these thoughts
   thoughts of callin' it off

oh you ready to go? hold up baby girl
   i'll get the check inna second
   i just realized i can't call you that cause i ain't claim and collect it
   girl why you holdin' out on me?

OF COURSE

not even really sure how you breaking my heart
   i wasn't even really, seriously attached from the start
   i mean i guess i'm a little addicted to feeling conflicted
   instead of just calling you
   asking if we could simply restart
   "simply restart?"
   you right - there's nothin' simple 'bout the matters of heart
   does it matter how long we stay out if we head back to my car?
   i wanna get to know you over chicken and fries
   trynna keep my eyes on ya eyes but they keep on driftin' to thighs
   of course i'm talkin' about the chicken..

of course
   you want reassurance straight from the source
   i'll tell you whassup, you tell me whassup - somehow we met with remorse
   i'm not even sure how i drove off course if i was only ever parked with you
   we ain't go nowhere far from the shores of the start
   so what's the matter with my heart?

Stagnant Heart

heavy is the softened heart
    for i carry the weight of water
    and i have always been clumsy.

i will not move
    therefore
    i will not shatter.

Fracturée

surprised i'm talkin'
   bit my tongue all my life
   held down teeth on taste buds
   never anything sweeter than strife

but it's so good to see you raven
   heard you're married now
   heard you lost the unborn
   on the phone with God for you now

but i can't hear you through the mist
   it's harder for me to remain sane
   no matter how long i look at you
   can't even hear you say my name

how far is everything from here?
   you got married before the world's sickness
   lost the unborn in high school
   my mind - trapped - dark thickness

i'll be born tomorrow
   we become friends yesterday

SOULPUNK

    i never said je t'aime
    should've been eight years ago today

my mind is splintered
    depression is unbound to time
    even when i was with my lady
    i think i was trapped under you all that time

Pink

pink
orchard blossom
a beautiful song
of dance
and deep
red

And All That She Showed Me In 24 Hours

and that morning
   you showed me your first smile of the day
   how lucky i was to have witnessed such a thing

and that afternoon
   you showed me the brightness of your laughter
   how lucky i was to have heard it

and that evening
   you showed me your love for the sun
   how lucky i was to have shared the moment

and that night
   you showed me the depth of your walls
   how lucky i was to have breathed with you.

Tethered Lust

tender kisses fill our hollow bodies with fire
   we could recognize each other in the darkness
   the indents in our fingers
   the scars from falls in our clumsy youth.

but we never have those conversations
   rather we recognize one another
   by scent and bites
   my lips or your thigh gap

one would believe
   our intimacy sparked the sun
   born in darkness
   to burn for eternity
   or so the night seems between us.

in you is the stairway to heaven
   i go there whenever you need me to
   whenever you tease me to
   whenever i yearn for you.

if i follow your voice

spoken softly
loudly
fiercely
i will conquer the earth in a single night.

and in the calm morning
   we will find each other again
   with no commitment
   no struggle
   no need for hassle
   but in stillness
   like a quiet, lakeside morning.

Down The Road

down the road
   thought i saw a man just like me
   down the road
   i know there's a man just like me

you, man down the road
   look at me
   i know the places you used to go

you, man down the road
   look at me
   i know the women you used to hold

you, man down the road
   look at me
   i know the jokes you you've once told

you, man down the road
   look at me
   i know all the prayers you behold
   look at me…
   and help

give me a hint -
   no, a way out of this hell
   i've seemed to have lost my key
   or maybe i never had one to begin with
   which is why i find myself so troubled now
   my mind wanders to the stage lights -
   a graceful bow
   and the house lights forever shut off.

Symphony of Doubt

the ground i walk
   riddled of shadows
   confuses me
   am i even moving at all?

do i chase the thrill of acting to be on screen
   so i can say to myself
   look
   i am living
   or do i truly love such a thing?

i have joys
   friends and family
   socialization
   even in isolation
   creating or consuming art

but everything is overwhelming me
   even the little things
   hundreds of tiny holes punctured into my sides
   sinking me further down into the sea
   will it swallow me?

or will God send a whale?

maybe He already has and i'm in it
   forced to battle my inner demons everyday to conquer them
   and when i've won over my guilt
   He'll release me from it

but where will i be spat up?
   in the reeds of depression?

i have been entangled for years now
   and i'm overgrown with aggression

self pity rules me
   destruction of self rules me
   anxiety rules me

what is my purpose?
   if i have offended You
   please forgive me
   and in the same breath
   please tell me
   what is my purpose?
   i've been distracting myself
   running from an awful truth

i'm in a spiral of sin and doubt
   uncertainty smells as thick as sauerkraut
   even these simple lines
   hold no light to our God vs man bout

SYMPHONY OF DOUBT

the only time i feel the ground is when my calves are burning
   my feet are aching
   or my toes are in the sand

how do i keep going like this
   if i'm just going to feel like this?

i've fled from therapy and churches
   the cost for both services
   is too high a price
   yet they both offer salvation
   one for the mind
   one for the soul
   but i have corrupted my mind
   and politics have corrupted my cross

every year i feel my mental
   crack and heal
   more and more
   trying to find a balance
   the meaning of staying alive
   so many whys
   how many wide eyes would be present
   if i...?
   never mind

my life
   it seems never full
   forever on the rise

oh look,

even the snake in the Garden
seems to have shed a tear for my crumbling lies

Fold Your Hands, My Son

I'm the shepherd and the sheep
   I'm the snow and the sleet
   I'm the spare and the street
   don't you dare forget Me

I'm the paper and the tree
   I'm the board and the brie
   I'm the bound and the free
   don't you dare forget Me

I'm the ship and the sea
   I'm the flower and the bee
   I'm the cup and the tea
   don't you dare forget Me

I'm the flat and the steep
   I'm the moon and the leap
   I'm the sow and the reap
   don't you dare forget Me

What I'd Do For Friends

a spider in your bathroom
   it may or may not disappear
   before my hand with the shoe appears

if i miss and we don't get it tonight
   trust, we'll get that bitch tomorrow
   with much more might

all for you.

a spider in my mind
   webbing traps my days and nights
   i cannot move to find the light

if joy and laughter escape me today
   trust, i will try finding it tomorrow
   an attempt at burying my sorrow

all for you.

yet, you tell me it's okay to not be okay
   but, my friends, this burden

WHAT I'D DO FOR FRIENDS

makes it hard to believe you.

Ça va, Raven?

   i woke up from a dream worried about you
      wondering if i could see you soon as tomorrow
      i'm hopin' that you forgive me
      and can help through the sorrow
      that i thought i left behind
      but i find it's harder to let go of the childhood strife
      in this life of mine
      but keep in mind
      this life proves much harder without you
      been seeing you in my dreams
      i'm worrying about you
      know you ran off to get married at a young age,
      but know i never had any doubts about you

 i still think about the last time we spoke in person
      said you found a career - you becoming a different person
      different version of yourself - a woman of the night
      plenty of women already there,
      surely you don't wanna join 'em right?
      'cause i know what was offered to you in this life
      but maybe its a chance to write somethin'
      better for yourself,

ÇA VA, RAVEN?

    better than the cards dealt

knew you since i was fifteen
    you always had an ace up your sleeve
    maybe there's somethin' better for you
    if you do decide to leave

but i can't even reach out
    'cause i deleted your number
    countless nights worrying 'bout you
    losing my slumber

remembering my first talent show
    when my poetry helped me speak
    remembering when you popped up
    and placed a kiss upon my cheek

never broke through that friend barrier
    for so long i've been an avid regret carrier

did my words ever hold any weight on you anyways?
    wonder if my words ever impacted your days,
    wonder if they ever impacted your sleeping habits,
    writing ways, ways that you lived your life
    or any of your days like you impacted mine,
    can't wrap my head around the possibility
    that you listened to me more than i did you
    and i'm left with the thought that maybe
    it was me that actually left you

alone

SOULPUNK

out here in a world so cold

maybe i wrecked you
    maybe i didn't reach out enough
    maybe back then or even now i've convinced myself i had enough
    maybe i'm the reason we fell out of touch
    maybe i'm part of the reason you found a career
    with a touch of lust

The Time Keeps Passing

the leaves keep turning
   the beard keeps growing
   the pain keeps piercing
   the wounds keep healing
   the rain keeps pouring
   the rivers keep drying
   the heart keeps pounding
   the eyes keep loving
   the lips keep locking

the yeast keeps rising
   the mind keeps dreaming
   the job keeps calling
   the moods keep swinging
   the fire keeps blazing
   the stars keep glowing
   the body keeps aging

the tears keep coming
   the crowd keeps clapping
   the music keeps playing
   the soul keeps grazing

SOULPUNK

   the lion keeps waiting

the sun keeps shining
   the friends keep waving
   the earth keeps spinning

the prayers keep sending
  ...

The Corners of My Mouth Shall Rise

when did i become too cool to laugh?
   the coolness has been pretentious
   my subconscious is full of bitter rage
   to crack a smile would be shameful
   it would be omitting my guilt and pains
   things i am not worthy of purging
   but such heavy burdens on my lips
   have silenced me with an unknown strength

have i not suffered enough?
   why must i punish myself every minute of my life?
   i will laugh today
   i will smile today
   i will find happiness in others and myself
   i will find happiness in a warm shower
   a warm bed
   things i have lost or taken for granted
   things i have been fearful of losing again

for wearing the crown of woe
   feels like playing it safe
   because i know that darkness all too well

and playing it safe in the abyss
has always been
a dangerous game

Holster

they shut down the basketball courts after that kid got shot...

i heard the bang
   paid no mind to it
   was blind -
   absent minded to it

i was walking down the street
   flashlights shined on me
   two cops eyed on me
   they asked "what're you doing out here?"
   going to a church across the street
   they i.d.'d me and let me be

another cop came up
   she quickly reached for her gun
   did she see someone's son?
   or assume that i was the one

who shot that kid on the basketball court...
   who shot that kid on the basketball court?

Scrape

i despise those that look down on depression
   as if it is a luxury
   as if it is asked for

for what i have is like walking around with a knife tied to my ankle

why am i so bedridden?
   so motionless?
   because i'm tired of hearing
   the scraping noise as i walk
   at least it is less of a nuisance
   when i am still

i become less and less,
   as the scrape becomes more and more
   something i've been told
   by preachers
   that i should be doing with God

i try to claim victory over it
   start doing things with my life
   and sometimes

SCRAPE

the noise is tuned out

then i hear it louder than ever
   wanting to take the knife
   and do the job of the reaper myself

at least i wouldn't hear it anymore
   feel it anymore
   tied to me

but then
   i would have never known my life
   without the scraping…

though i know
   something is *afoot*, ha
   maybe it isn't a rope and knife

maybe it is a snake around my ankle,
   hissing in the sound of a scrape,
   making me search for the rattle
   instead of meaning
   as it feeds off my joys

or maybe,
   it is the lion
   sinking his teeth into my flesh,
   trying to drag me away…

how will i ever know anything,
   dear God,

if you do not SPEAK?

Oh Brother, Where Is Our God?

prayers and hard times
   a combo like chicken fried
   mash potato sides
   but the chicken ain't that damn good
   somebody lied

and so i'm out here eating my guilt
   done hard labor but this the house anxieties built
   clumsy since lil kid - look at all the shit i done spilt
   trynna convince myself it ain't my fault the world on tilt

as i reflect i wish the love was stronger back then
   animosity in the air man fuck it we men

it's easy to be angry towards shit that i don't understand
   especially when i'm hearing everything via phone call firsthand
   "listen this ain't what i planned,
   but ask ya mans if he got a gun,
   you'll understand"
   how imma put a gun in ya hand?

"stop asking me questions sean - these mothafuckas loosenin' my lock,

    too many mothafuckas to count that's why ya brotha need a glock,
    been arguin with stupid niggas ever since you left the block,
    ain't even workin' no more - all i do is count with the clocks towards death,
        but i'll be damned if i breathe my last breath to some bitch ass niggas,
        tell ya boys to slide a burner so i can dump on niggas"

maybe you just trippin' - what would happen if some shit go south?
    if you killed a man and the cops found out from word of mouth?

that's just two accessories
    now momma gotta call multiple directories to talk to both of her sons
        we ain't never been about guns
        always heard the shots but we ain't never been them ones

but what's really goin' on in my mind is if you pointed it at ya self
    knew you was suicidal since high school - been there myself
    as i write this realize we never talked about the feelings we felt
        when our mental health was taking a toll cause the cards we was dealt

anxiety is boomin'
    hearing you scared, yellin' at me on the other end of the line
    is death really fuckin' loomin'?

how the fuck could i decide?
    i withheld somethin' i maybe coulda provided and on the other hand
    you prolly coulda died

riddled with emotions and i'm still choosing the logical

OH BROTHER, WHERE IS OUR GOD?

   decisions in life is fucked up man shit is comical
   exactly why i wish i could get away - somewhere illogical
   just be far away like the distance is astronomical

but if keep runnin'
   keep runnin'
   KEEP RUNNIN'
   KEEP A RUN-RUN-RUNNIN'
   shit i'll never face an obstacle

every night just wishin' i was at sea
   every day dreamin' of a bigger, better me
   head poundin', nightmares just keep eggin' me on
   and momma gettin' busy i don't think she pray for me

every damn day fightin' just to keep the green
   every day grindin' so my pockets don't flee
   hard for me to sleep- close my eyes- i see neon
   every damn day i feel less and less free

is this anxiety?
   panic attack, cold sweat
   is this anxiety?
   titanium around my neck
   is this anxiety?
   "all the time gotta watch my back"
   is this anxiety?
   prayin' that he don't get whacked…

Dreadful Sighs

*these days
i sigh to get the feeling out of my chest
but it never escapes
it has found its place
resting upon my shame.*

No Crutch For Love

wipe away your sweat
   fade into my chest

the lingering of our last touch
   still replays in my mind

it peaked at passion for you
   it turned into a need for me

tasking you with a simple job
   do what it takes to remove the pain

the redness in your cheeks
   a blush covered by laughter

makes me regrettably
   recall the lighter shades of your walls

you called me by other titles
   and still convinced me you knew my name

for every time i see you on the morrow

SOULPUNK

    the night prior is yearner's eve

i am the sailor pulled by the call of the sea
    one would believe my ship was sinking

never is the word love uttered
    there is a different desire in the air

and as i arrive in your presence
    my mind is already made up

tomorrow i will be a Believer
    but tonight i will believe in you

Spares

so familiar
   when you walk my way
   are you on your way?
   where do you lay?

some neat hat trick you pulled off there
   you can't find your underwear
   i can't find that piece of my mind
   do you know we don't have spares?

i'll send for you when i find them
   long as you send for me when you find me.
   ...
   haven't seen you in days
   do you know how much your memory weighs?

heavy like the words i love you, maybe
   no, not that
   heavy like a newborn baby, maybe
   no, not that

i can't stay up too much longer — waiting

i need that piece to get good rest
my friends keep asking me why i am tired.

Sand

you're like sand
   endlessly slipping through my fingers
   you've been evasive
   since the day i met your lips

your mind started moving in a different direction
   like tidal waves
   since the day we kissed

i wonder if we've seen the blue dawn of this day before
   it feels like the second time you've killed my heart
   the second time we met at the start

and you've always ran away
   because i refused to grow -
   to change
   to move at a different pace
   i ask
   what is the price of love?
   and what does it pay?
   you ask what my fears are made of?
   and what do they say?

i'd rather find out from myself
   than find out from you

you could end all of me with a sweet kiss
   or a swift cut
   graceful eyes that kiss gently if you stare at them from the right angle
   and hidden at your waist
   a cutlass
   your soft fingers hover over
   waiting to cut out my love
   and watch it dangle

i'm distracted by your beauty
   your vocality
   your kindness
   your lustfulness

i remove your jacket
   you remove yours
   i remove my pants
   you remove yours
   you remove your shirt
   i remove mine -
   sparks die

falling as lust in the dark
   the shadows warm the walls in the moonlight
   or maybe it wasn't as pure
   yet the glow was streetlight

SAND

on our backs side by side
   we stare at the illuminated ceiling
   inhaling the hot, sinful air
   but neither of us care
   my cross hugged your chest
   as your nails hugged my back
   just moments ago

it must have felt like a mirror for you
   from the side eye
   i could tell you reflected
   is this the woman you wanted to be?
   you saw my heart
   you saw the way i treated love
   and lust
   and saw no difference maybe

you found
   in the dark with my heart
   more of me than i showed in broad day

i didn't comfort you after
   no kiss
   nor hold
   no bliss
   before you made up your mind

you found your reason to escape
   the repetitive bed sharing
   to the emotion bending
   sexcapade of young life -

from my faults of misconstruing love with lust

sleep was not present that night
   loneliness was
   you left earlier than usual that night

the wounds around my chest
   started to bleed through my shirts over time
   i was restless
   covered in my own faults in the night time

in the mirror
   someone i don't know
   but wish to be better than,
   grows

scars around my heart
   you took it
   and i didn't know why...
   but you gave it back

i catch a fleeting feeling of your fingers presence sometimes
   in these sheets
   that for a time weren't just mine

i question my purpose as a man
   in this world
   in this life

why do i succumb
   so easily

SAND

   with little fight
   to lust?

and on the other hand
   so harshly
   with much resistance
   to love?

i fear reality
   much more than fiction
   because at least in the dark
   under covers with a midnight lover
   i don't have to be afraid of the morning
   i don't have to worry about how i'm going to love you
   with all of my strength today
   no plans to pray for your life today
   no thoughts on how to make you smile within the bounds of me today
   yet, here i am
   worrying about you; the door to love was cracked in my heart
   the light was on
   you were standing in the door way
   i ask
   were you waiting for me?
   or waiting for me to fall back asleep
   so you could,
   in the stillness of the night,
   flee?

i worry
   there are no lies between your eyes and my soul

i didn't want to worry about how to introduce you
   the right way
   to my friends of life
   my family of life
   my individual way of life

you tried to wake me
   not flee
   you wanted to come into this world of mine
   and stay
   and yet
   when you came and sat on my bed
   i turned away

ashamed of you
   i wanted you in secrecy
   you fought to get into my life
   and i said no

oh
   how my worry deserves no pity
   how my dreaded hours thinking of your existence
   in my bed
   on my couch
   in your kitchen
   deserves no remorse

am i worth forgiving?
   am i worth your hours of this one life
   as you are worth mine?

SAND

did i find you
   a shining diamond
   in my bleak love life
   or did God
   reveal you to me?

a beauty to love
   before i could grow into a proper man
   with the appropriate tools
   and the right lessons learned
   to take care of her?
   with the right affection
   and intelligence
   to love her?

what a cruel thing from the inside out

to reveal an angel
   a sinful man cannot properly appreciate
   because he has not learned yet
   what love really is
   and how to think with the correct head

what a way to break the soul
   my mirror
   has never been the same

because it is broken
   and so it seems the man
   but
   therein lies the path

    the given pieces
    to reconstruction

the rebirth
    the comprehension
    the walking path revealed by the cracks
    the ice lake finally has a line to avoid
    it is no longer a self-reflection of pity
    but through interpretation
    meditation
    healing
    and reeducation
    it is a path to conquer fear
    to put down fallacies
    to evade defiling urges
    and to welcome,
    in its fullest capacity,
    achievable in this one life,
    romantic love.

the kind of love that resurrects
    the soul within

to welcome it
    to accept it
    and to embrace it

but now that i understand
    some part of this mystery
    i watch you
    packed up your feelings

SAND

    and like sand
    slip through the cracks of my life

i try to grasp you
    but you evade my attempt
    and i'm stuck wondering where you are
    while the tiniest bit of your residue
    tightly clings to me
    and all that i own.

I Should Let You Go, But…

there is a depth within you
that i must accept
i may never get to know

but i'd rather try to know you anyway
than have to face that goddamn mirror
alone

Still Both of Yours

i stand on the beach after a run
   i close my eyes and still see the sun
   who am i as a son?
   i loved that girl
   i hurt that boy
   i had my fun…
   i still have my fun
   i played that guitar
   got drunk at that bar
   my feelings are on the run…
   why on the run?
   i pray on the earth
   you cried at my birth
   i'm still one…
   i'm still one of yours…
   i never moved my mountains
   i made you cry fountains
   am i still your son?
   what is your love?
   the flight of doves
   start as low as the ground,
   go as high as the sun?

you cast love beyond the sun…
i'm in tune with my heart because of you
i'm in tune with my culture because of you
when God said let there be light
He created the both of you.

i am your baltimore son,
   i am your california man.

i am still both of yours.

Requiem For A Bluebird

"don't quit your day job"
   you don't have to tell me
   that i have debts and rents
   a car note and car dents
   dress shirts i never bothered to buy
   until i needed a solidified nine-to-five
   haven't worn polo shirts
   since working at the movie theater

struggling to remain awake
   behind this computer monitor
   tasked with organizing files
   that end up looking better than my room
   but i come to
   out of the blue of the machine
   by a thud against the window
   and i catch the cause of the noise

a frail little thing
   wings expanded and flapping
   before it crashed into my pane
   my castle of posterity

or so it should be
i ask my colleague if she'd heard or seen it
"no, nothing"
i turn to the monitor and ponder upon my reflection

"don't quit your day job"
you don't have to remind me
that these three to four cups
of bitter, bitter black coffee
gets the debts and rents paid
maybe a little creamer this time
now it's a bittersweet savior
the aroma resuscitates my mind

i spy a little frail thing
flying by my immovable castle
its beak crashes against the window
the first time i see the beginning and end
why, my friend, are you just like the other?
my colleague has missed nature versus man again
i should be worried about the winged sorrow
but i'm saving my anxiety for my six-month review

trying to balance my job and art
suit and tie versus silver screen dreams
all the while my foundation is full of theatre gleams
i find no drive for the gym
i'm gaining weight behind this monitor and blue light
my office swivel chair that caters to remaining seated
taking naps on break in the psychiatrist's office
dreams telling me to remain or escape

REQUIEM FOR A BLUEBIRD

"don't quit your day job"
   i adhere to the holy modern scripture
   if i move to los angeles now
   i'll have the equivalent of a 15th-century french peasant
   six livre and a fucking turkey leg
   trading my castle of posterity for chance
   under the reigning dominance of lord angeles
   its beast will devour me if i falter

i arrive early to the machine
   the black savior pouring into my cup
   i gaze out the lunch patio window
   to take in the day nature has presented
   but on the ground of the patio i spot a little frail thing
   my dear friend, your wings are motionless
   your charm has escaped you
   why have you fallen before me like the others?

the ladies of the office are coming into the building
   i hear the jingling of keys, laughter, the rumbling of iced coffees
   my mind does not want you to rot inside the trash can
   i cannot carry you out of the office past them
   the people pleaser in me will not crush their morning
   swept into my dustpan - i drop you over the edge
   i watch your flightless body fall two stories
   crashing into the dirt at the foot of my castle of posterity

"don't quit your day job"
   yes i know that mother and father
   yes i understand that brother and sister
   i must keep my dignity by holding a job

    biweekly paychecks and a roof over my head
    pto and sick time are synonymous
    use them wisely for filming and playing dead
    because monday through friday is the real zombie

i pass the ladies on their way in
    pretending as if the little frail thing is non-existent
    acting has paid off - i hardly notice without a stage
    i move with haste outside and find you by a tree
    why did i even come down here to see you?
    i wish your wings worked as well as my dreams
    no matter - i must return to the machine
    my castle of posterity relies upon a good six-month review

sitting across from my supervisors
    they tell me i've scored excellently
    "this is the highest anyone could achieve on their review"
    but the tears forming are not their tears of joy
    health services are being met with statewide budget cuts
    my position has therefore been made "redundant"
    as the perfectly formatted paper states before me
    and i must take the redundancy on the chin

"don't quit your day job"
    i didn't have a chance to this time
    i've quit countless times in the past
    not enough money or black coffee
    not worth the risk or not fulfilling
    now it is a different look - a different conversation
    when i tell you i had no control over being laid off
    just like the characters i love on the silver screen

my castle of posterity crumbles before me
   though it was never my castle to begin with
   not my rug, which was yanked from underneath me
   my ass could not spare me of the pain from falling back
   too many "me's", "my's", and "i's"
   the office space felt like it was meant– good for me
   or maybe i just got too good at pretending
   i should have listened to the messenger who saw right through me

what, blue bird, did you so desperately want to deliver?
   was it repetition - the meaning of insanity?
   would it have freed me from this caged circle of nine-to-five?
   were you telling me to risk everything in this castle light
   perchance to live in flight?
   or was it for you what it was always growing to be for me?
   seeing our reflections in monitors and windows
   only to detest what our eyes happened to see?

War

war.
   you're here,
   you're there,
   you're not everywhere,
   because sometimes i escape you.

though sleep is like a stranger to love.
   i want you,
   but not yet,
   because something is keeping me away.

insomnia.
   but, steady is the mind when it finally falls asleep.
   images, voices, movements-
   a french woman meets me in my dream.

i am more wowed by her presence,
   than her of me.
   walking by her side, i tell her
   "your accent is lovely"
   but she's on the move
   and paying no mind to me.

WAR

i awake,
    brain vibrating from a short rest.
    the feelings inside are long gone,
    leaves me to wonder where are the rest?

daily life seems so connected,
    and yet, everything is
    down,
    up.

good news,
    then bad news to make you grateful for *at least i got good news*.

then the worst in due time,
    the worst inside,
    nothing in your heart but wishes,
    the worst parts of your voice overriding your mind.

just get out of bed.
    just get to work.
    just do it.
    just go.
    get. up.
    do something.

war is not that simple.

there's no pedal for the gas.
    no wheel to steer my mind.
    no water to grow the grass.

the bombs in the distance is self-hate closing in.
   the bullets in the ground are lies i let bleed in.
   the church in ruin is my religion spreading thin.

i am already awake,
   but before i even open my eyes,
   the lion reminds me that i'm wrestling with him.

roaring inside my mind and heart.
   slashing me with claws of doubt,
   claws of self destruction,
   claws of depression.

his jaw forms around my head,
   but i move before he can bite.

the knife walks around in my contemplation,
   but i come to before i slice.

the price is not worth the endless slumber.
   but day in, day out
   war is my partner.

the only thing stagnant,
   the only thing rampant.

the war has gone on longer than my thoughts of romanticization.
   the war has gone on longer than my time in conversation.

longer than i've been around my mother
   longer than i've been around a lover.

WAR

some days the war is not with a lion,
   but with a french woman in my dreams.
   the quiet war on the inside that no one sees.
   tucked underneath like pant seams.

sometimes i thank God
   the knife and the lion
   didn't have a good enough reason.

the war in me is not all me,
   but yet the pressure,
   the scale of power,
   feels like a separate entity
   two versions of myself
   me and the impostor
   fighting over control
   of the same vessel.

i wish you understood that it's not easy,
   but you can't understand.

no matter how much you read about the lion,
   the french woman,
   me.

you will never understand not having enough elbow room inside to breathe,
   to speak and say no.

you will never understand not knowing what goes where up here.
   you will never understand the war of fighting for your life against

yourself.

you see,
    there is no man trying to kill me,
    unless he wakes up in the mirror.

there is no man trying to suffocate me,
    unless he doesn't feel like coming up for air.

there is no man trying to isolate me,
    unless he pushes everyone away.

there is no man trying to torture me,
    unless he welcomes his regrets like a wildfire.

before you tell me to get out of bed,
    to get over it,
    to stop acting this way,
    to be happy,
    to make a living,
    because it is what everyone does,
    or to simply pray it away,
    ask yourself —
    how much can a man at war do in a day?

And I Avoided The Song She Might've Sung

it's been a long time
   a long while
   a long sigh

i missed you
   but i won't say how much
   or for how long
   there's no right way to right the wrongs of unspoken words
   unsung songs

i'm ashamed to say
   that i don't have the energy to keep up
   with your warm smile today
   one that could warm the entire amazon
   the unfortunate tears i could bring you
   would add salt to that river

i would love to be genuine
   but i'm afraid -
   i'm not sure -
   unsure how to -

not able to find a seat for you inside

how about we just stick to the surface?
   don't ask me about purpose
   ask me how work is
   easy conversations we can manage to boredom

would you break,
   ask me what my deal is,
   or ease away,
   save yourself from the surface stuff?

how much could i bullshit you over coffee?
   over teas i don't mind drinking because you like them
   over drinks at my favorite bar
   over my house late after game night has ended with my friends -
   before you ask me something that you hope will crack me open?

i hope you do(n't).

A Quiet Harm

will i ever let the petals of sweet flowers
   bloom and fall where they may,
   or must i always continue marching on
   with the ripping of nature?

such a subtle, simple act of destruction
   i have learned as a boy

Blood Betrayal

his mind
  it's broken
what?
he hears-
"i hear voices"
people talking shit about him
"a wolf"
that's why he lost so many jobs
"i hear peoples souls judging me"
and now he's been drinking every day
"they know i hear them, they taunt me"
smoking cigarettes, barely eating, yelling at me
"i heard our mother and sister cry out for help"
sean, you hear me?
"the wolf"
he scares me, i never know when he's gonna—
"let me fuckin' stay here nigga"
snap
"i'm the only brother you got"
he grabbed me last week, my arm, i called the cops
"at the end of the day, all we got is family"
the people at the hospital said he declined help

"i don't want to lose my mind sean"
he's so selfish and he don't care about nobody else
"help me sean"
let me pray for you
sometimes he just make me want to kill myself
"why that nigga talking so loud on the phone?"
what?
"slow down, imma beat his ass"
he's not bothering anyone
sean, you have to let him go
"aye can i borrow some money for the liquor store?"
you shouldn't have let him drink
it's our last supper together
"you my servant nigga, you here to serve"
we're all here to serve
"had you and my mom cook for me like bitches"
i chose to cook for you cause you're my brother
he's not your problem sean
just keep praying and let me know what happens
"i'm sorry about the other day"
you can't... you can't stay here
"why didn't you just say that then?"
i did
are you nice to sean?
what? yeah, that's been my boy since high school
i don't know what to do
you need to call the cops and say he's trespassing
here, have a drink friend
i'm the only one that's never called the cops—
"where you at?"
on him... my mom, dad and sister have

it's not your fault, he's just gotta go, look at you
i'm gonna pick him up in the morning
"whassup sean"
where are you?
she left sean, she's already heading out here
what? we were gonna find him a shelter with services
she been driving all night to virginia, she sounded tired
i can only give you a week
he's been there, what, two weeks now?
almost three
if he doesn't go on his own, you gotta kick 'em out
"we can do it together nigga"
he turned down his meds from the hospital
"i guess i'll just get somethin to drink
and ask one of them in the field if i can sleep in their tent"
you can just get into a shelter or a facility
"shut the fuck up or imma beat the shit outta you"
he's threatening you now?? call the cops
i just want to give him a chance
"what nigga? you wanna fight sean?"
*no shane, i don't want to fight, i'm just trynna fuckin' help you
and you can't fuckin' see that*
you been spending a lot of time at the track
it's the only place i can think
hey, so you really want to join the air force?
yes, i want to leave as soon as possible
okay
today's the day he leaves, let me know what happens
if he left earlier to one of the places i found for him, he could've got a bed
he left at 10pm? where'd he go??
i don't know, he didn't even take the phone charger

it's your brother
you can open it
"walk to the store with me"
i'm busy
"sean, you can't just walk to the damn store?"
shane i'm busy
"nigga come on, i'm your brother, just walk to the store. i been out all night and day, you can't leave the house for a minute?"
alright damn
"i ain't even slept yet"
you could've gotten a bed at a shelter
"i'm not goin' back to those fuckin' places"
i don't know what you want from me shane
"you and your roommate was talkin shit about me huh?"
what? we weren't even talking about you
"you don't know what those places are like. i was walking all fuckin' night nigga. we been in dangerous places before but this shit was different."
that's not my fault

BANG.
his balled fist meets the right of my chin —
suddenly, a forgotten adrenaline kicks in.

are you serious?
are you fuckin serious?
"yeah nigga"
put ya shit down. put ya shit down.
"come on, sean. come on."

we strike each other. make each other bleed.

SOULPUNK

fists kicks grapples
hooks jabs weaves
headbutts shaking pleas
squared up in the middle of the street
i was the only one trying to fuckin' help you

My Cousin Named Cultural Stigma

said to my fam "you shouldn't trust that shit
    trauma and medicine ain't somethin you should meddle in
    it's a fictitious thing - they only want to make a profit off you
    get you hooked to whatchamacallit and don't come lookin for you

pray about it
    be about it
    it'll resolve itself"
    but that equation never made sense since i was twelve
    'cause is he trynna solve him or just solve for him?
    is he the solution or part of the problem?
    my brothers mind will meet a thief and the thief will try to rob 'em

asked for a gun to keep the thief outside his door
    take us back to safer, simpler times, freshly mopped floors
    never even seen the signs, eyes was never opened or
    never was educated - we ain't know what to look for

Brothers In Spring(time)

march
   i am not ready
   anxious
   found you hidden in my room
   crouched
   drinking
   "hey sean"

maybe at a different time in life i could have helped
   but i'm broke
   this is not my roof
   not my shelter
   living in borrowed quarters
   enough bus fare to get to work
   3 hours waiting for a bus to get home
   food for the job
   and maybe at home
   if i'm lucky (disciplined)
   all the while you denied your diagnosis
   and stopped taking your medication

you are everything i can't stand to be around

BROTHERS IN SPRING(TIME)

and you are everything i love
you've thrown away a lot of your life
i suppose my anger isn't justified entirely
i threw away a great amount of my days and nights

maybe it wasn't anger at all
   because when i saw you
   my mind shifted
   and i wanted to flee immediately

flee from the world i knew
   the walls of jericho were already crumbling
   the life that i built suddenly ripping apart even more
   too instant to stop it
   everything i did then fanned the flames

i left you in that room i called home
   and called the army
   hoping to find a new one
   tearing, not running, away from you
   like a shredding of construction paper
   because i saw shreds of myself in you that day

so i worked on myself everyday
   walking
   jogging
   running that track across the street from "home"
   for hours and hours
   something i hadn't done with so much conviction
   and purpose
   since high school

i'd find you on that track
   in my way some meters down
   smoking a cigarette
   waiting for me to pass so you could talk to me

it was there that i spoke up for myself
   but in speaking up
   i slowly became indifferent
   and you did too

animosity strengthened along our path
   quicker than a rose bush could prick us
   challenging each other
   arguing over territory
   over the past we recalled so differently
   over the current situation presented
   over our own histories of suicidal tendency
   which we both resented.

april
   i am ready
   weight training
   united states air force security forces
   instead of army infantry
   i was so determined to shorten my mile time
   i broke down how quick and steady i'd need to be
   for every quarter mile
   how much weight i'd have to burn off
   to pass the upcoming test

the day had come for you to leave

BROTHERS IN SPRING(TIME)

    you wanted no part in a mental facility
    or a shelter
    that i hoped could provide you housing in due time
    nor did you want no part in your medicine
    i begged you
    i called on God
    His phone must've rang a thousand times
    and when He answered
    He told me this one is for me

why did it fall into my hands?
    everyone said to call the police to get you to leave
    but you're my brother
    and i trusted your word when you said "i'll leave"
    i just wanted to help you fight this disease
    such a thin line between who i know you to be
    and schizophrenia
    that i didn't think of anything else
    besides defending myself
    when you punched me

i lost my grip on the love i was holding onto
    adrenaline spoke for me
    i looked at you
    and it was like…
    you saw me as someone else
    or maybe i was just never in your cross hairs
    i could never forget that look on your face
    and the feeling of betrayal in my gut

"are you serious?"

...
"are you fucking serious?"
"yeah nigga"
"put your shit your down… put your shit down"

we squared up
   middle of the street
   asphalt
   the same asphalt we'd race each other on as kids
   dirty socks with holes and toes poking out
   'cause we'd run faster without shoes on
   tiny bits of glass from smashed bottles
   the places we used to run
   dumpster, to the end of apartments ahead, and back
   our sister was faster than me
   but you were faster than her
   i always tried to catch you
   never quite could though
   always tried to be brave like you
   like in 8th grade
   my best friend wanted to drown herself
   at the small lake behind your high school
   and i spent hours talking her out of it
   only for our family to be mad when i got home
   and you scorned me for being brave
   everyone scorned me for being so stupid
   so stupid as to try and save someone
   because i was black and she was white
   so the question wasn't "what would you do
   if she followed through?"
   rather, it was "if you were the last one to be with her

BROTHERS IN SPRING(TIME)

   what would they do to you
   if she followed through?"

and here
   in the street
   we circle each other
   tension smothered in angst and heartbreak
   fists in the air
   outwardly - our faces were of hate
   but inward…
   deep inside…
   it was years of misunderstandings
   years of wanting the best for each other,
   and watching each other shit on our futures
   years of closed mouths and rarely exclaiming "i love you"
   holding each other to impossible standards

just weeks ago we held each other in tears
   "i don't want to lose my mind, sean"
   now we're fighting out of fear

i know you're challenging my manhood
   you never thought i had it in me
   you thought all our lives that i was too weak
   too insecure
   too meek
   too much of a pussy
   a coward
   ignorant
   arrogant

selfish
materialistic

to live.
   to be on my own.
   to take on life without you,
   without the 4 us being together like old times.
   you, me, mom, sis -
   dad here and there throughout our lives physically
   and a voice faraway over the phone,
   but those were old times.

and i live,
   as i swing at you,
   and you swing at me,
   connecting punches
   kicks
   head butts
   grapples
   by God, i live
   and i scream
   "I WAS THE ONLY ONE TRYING TO FUCKIN HELP YOU"

i traded in our mother's cross
   for a fight
   as the chain it hangs on
   lays snapped in the street

went from you teaching me how to box
   to kicking off my slippers
   and fighting you in my socks

BROTHERS IN SPRING(TIME)

our kid selves watched us fight from the curbs
   across from each other
   they wondered
   "how did we get here?"

and they ran away from us
   hoping,
   in another life,
   to get it right.

the present us,
   the hurt men,
   walked away bruised.
   i looked at myself in the mirror,
   i spat blood in the bathroom sink,
   eye swelling,
   lip busted.
   still not knowing who the fuck is in my mirror.
   did i betray you?

i didn't see you after that,
   i jumped out of the little sleep i could get for weeks,
   severely anxious that you wanted to kill me because you weren't yourself
   and i had given you a pocket knife that you asked for
   to protect yourself the day before,
   and mom called to tell me you finally checked yourself into a facility,
   instead of aimlessly roaming the streets
   just hours after we fought.

end of april

i am still ready
my body is put through the gauntlet
united states air force PT
all i've been training for
willing to give up my life
even the stage and art that i live and breathe
just to get away
wearing shades the whole time
hid my black eye from the men and women in uniform

and after,
i sat on the bench with the sergeant
catching my breath
giving my body a break
shades on
staring out into the distance…
"we'll have another session next wednesday…"
i didn't hear much he said
i couldn't
all i heard was your voicemail the night after we fought
telling me over and over again that you did it
just to see if i could "stand up" for myself…
"let me get out of here before my girlfriend gives me hell.
take care wade. see you next week."
"thank you sergeant."

i thought all of my walls had fallen already
but my mind shifted again
and behold,
the last wall fell.

BROTHERS IN SPRING(TIME)

may
   i am not ready
   i thought that i could finally fly
   running away to the air force
   to trade in this pain for another
   but i gave it up
   maybe i wasn't strong enough
   or maybe i didn't see a reason to flee anymore since you left
   i wanted so badly to gain wings
   i was willing to sacrifice the stage
   my freedom
   my body
   willing to turn to the flag instead of God
   because it seemed He could not be bothered
   but the fight changed me
   knocked me back into a spiraling descent of my own ignored chaos
   just as much as i changed when i saw you waiting in my room weeks
ago.

i used to mourn you
   and try to save you
   in my dreams…
   but now when i dream of you
   all we do is argue,
   fight,
   or i am begging you not to attack me again.
   that moment between us
   radicalized even my subconscious of you.
   why?

we do not understand each other,

nor the power of the mind,
the power of grief and love
masked by hate and fear.

there is nowhere for me to run.
   why must the man i love the most
   hurt me like no other?

A Reflection

You say You made everyone
   every hair
   inch tick trait
   personality and physical
   mapped our lives -
   death
   and inbetween
   our birth date

then You made me too observant
   too quiet sensitive insecure
   afraid nervous introverted
   to see things play out
   non-interventional
   non-confrontational
   to silence offenders
   You made me a bystander
   to others
   and to my own
   discomfort pain wickedness
   fears
   You made me too wrathful

SOULPUNK

    unforgiving merciless
    ignorant to setting things straight
    for the good of the world around me
    and for myself

i grew up in a family of lecturers
    so i grew to listen
    rather than speak
    and i am still searching for my voice

have You had Yours all this time
    or are You just like me?

Talk To Me (About Your World)

"do you remember the first time you felt your heart beat?"
   it was the first time i ran out of breath
   "as a child?"
   yes, as a child.
   "how about in your teens?"
   the first time i fell in love.
   "did it work out?"
   i never told her.

"that sounds sweet and all, but are you hiding something?"
   nothing to hide, i'm an open book.
   "nothing?"
   everything, everything to hide.
   "why?"
   have you seen my world?

what it could do to a stranger,
   rather, what it can do to someone you love?

"you wouldn't risk anything if everything was out there"
   sure, let me tell all the women i ever loved how i felt
   let me tell my father and mother i hid the scar on my wrist for years

let me tell God everything i think is hidden from Him
let me tell my closet friends i gave up on therapy and still get suicidal
you hear how ridiculous that sounds?

"you are suffering"
   no i'm not
   "there is goodness here,
   but you are too angry to see it"
   it's not my fault
   "sure it is, and it isn't"
   the fuck is that supposed to mean?
   "it's not supposed to mean anything"
   just that everything that happens is meant for me huh?
   "you're not the only soul on your planet that feels like this"
   like what?

like what??
   hello?
   HELLO!?
   who else feels like this
   sore, but can't find the spot
   torn between wanting to live and rot
   all the pain would be easier if i just forgot
   where it all
   came from...

"it comes from being human"

but why? WHY do we suffer the things we suffer?
   God does not show mercy on all of us,
   and yet a father will be cursed if he does not show mercy on his

TALK TO ME (ABOUT YOUR WORLD)

child?
  WHY?

"because if you believe in Him
    then you must also believe that a mistake was made
    a grave, but honest mistake
    so learning had to be done
    and you have to find it in your heart to forgive it
    otherwise, don't ask anyone else for forgiveness
    when you tell or show them your truths

don't ask your mother, who raised you the best she could
    don't ask your father, whom you bare resemblance with
    don't ask your lovers, when you hurt them too much
    don't ask your friends, when you betray them
    don't ask God, when your whole life is sin
    don't ask your sister, when you ignore her calls
    don't ask your brother, when you've kicked him out

you are not the only one suffering
    for suffering is humanity's burden to bear
    not one man's"

what about Jesus?
    "His own creation killed Him
    do you think He stopped weeping after He died?
    do you not think He sometimes weeps alone on the throne
    unable to control His emotions
    and ultimately unable to control His world?

you have free will

because He knew He'd be tired
and so your world is tired, too"
so what are we to do?
"you keep moving"
why? knowing there will always be more pain?
"who knows? maybe He does, maybe He doesn't"

"but there is beauty in the unknown
   the consciousness of all humans
   the laughter of humanity
   the surrendering act of falling in love
   platonically and romantically
   the mind is so powerful you don't even fully understand it

you have allowed people and yourself to make you angry
   and you harbor it as if they are lucky you don't show it
   but what has happened when all the harboring
   is released on someone who barely pushed one button?
   you've hurt them
   every
   single
   time
   and yet, you say you are the victim?

you are all victims of something
   but the one thing that connects all of you
   is the cycle of life

you are all born students
   forced to learn the laws of the world
   and forced to redeem humanity time and time again

TALK TO ME (ABOUT YOUR WORLD)

    and you should not blame your mothers for birthing you

for women alone could end mankind
   but they have not
   they have given mankind every chance to better itself
   bringing a child in
   hoping they are the change the world needs
   no matter what atrocities have occurred
   a child was born through it
   and yet,
   if there were not so much division
   so much hatred and vitriol
   everyone would stop and stare to see the new life
   no matter the race
   religion
   creed
   no matter that living thing

they would all stop and wonder
   oh, there goes another little one
   i think i have hope for them

they would be reminded"
   reminded of what?
   "that they are born out of suffering
   in hopes that they find something to cling onto
   to prove the strength of humanity
   to prove they know the true meaning of love
   or maybe something more
   universal or divine
   Godly or unknown

you are not angry at birth
   no
     you do not cry out of the hatred of being born
     you cry because you have entered a new world
     a world outside of the womb
     where it was just you and your mother
       distant hellos from outside her belly like shooting stars
       and here you are, landing on earth
       finding your footing in the wilderness

do you not understand what you are feeling now?"
   no, i still don't. are there others that really feel this, too?
   "i will tell you again, you are not alone"
   but i am
   "why?"
   why am i alone?
   "yes"
   because no matter what, it will always just be me
   "you will have to forgive yourself one day
   for allowing yourself to believe that
   and you will have to hold out hope that you are wrong"

forgiveness,
   what a load of shit

"do you really believe that?
   ...
   you had a dream of losing one of your best friends dogs
   you cried out to him in the daylight of the woods
   over and over and over again
     waiting until you heard four legs sprinting through the dry leaves

TALK TO ME (ABOUT YOUR WORLD)

you must have yelled his name 20 times
waiting for an answer
and he did not return
no barking
no wailing
no, the leaves did not rustle
they sat quiet — not even disturbed by the wind
nothing —
you screamed for him
begged for him to come running back
because you could not bare to confront
the fact
that you lost him
that you let him go
and you knew, in the dream, that you would again
find yourself begging for her forgiveness
just as you did in reality
some years ago

tell me now how it is a load of shit
   that even in your dreams
   you are so afraid to deeply hurt someone

you had dreams of your brother dying for years
   walking downstairs in a suit and tie crying
   knowing it was for his funeral
   him being bitten by a snake and falling off a cliff
   others you can't even remember
   and the one time you did save him
   was when he wasn't around you as much anymore

you pulled him out of the water
   gave him cpr
   and you watched his chest closely, quietly, madly
   until
   he
   breathed
   and now you struggle to forgive him
   for doing what you have done to countless others

you ask what the suffering is for
   maybe it is so the word *save* can exist
   what if you are here to save one another
   everyday
   see how long you can save each other?"

from what?
   "from yourselves"
   but we will eventually die
   "it is not saving to live forever
   it is saving to last forever
   without you
   it is a sacrifice everyone must make
   that is the burden humanity bears together
   and through that burden is the passing of love
   from generation to generation
   but some cannot see that
   their anger has spoiled their soul like rotten meat
   and they march along this planet
   with pride in front and fire behind them

and so it is a cycle"

TALK TO ME (ABOUT YOUR WORLD)

is that fair?
"if you believe in God
ask Him is it fair He died for humanity
and the ones who continue to burn the world
would likely crucify Him today
nothing is fair
so it is your job as a human being to be fair
a simple balance
you created fairness
just as you created injustice
you created life
just as you created death
yet, both come naturally
humans shouldn't be cruel about it
but some just are
unfortunately you share the whole planet with them"

so is that everything?
"no"
what's left?
"finding your place in your world
even when it screams it wants you dead
even when you scream the same
you have to sift through the pains
to either find the love
or create it —
forgiving those who look like you
and finding a unified way
to resist and extinguish the flames

because

life must go on"

why?
   ...
  "why not?"

God, Won't You End Me

i'd like to barter
   this weight of water

holding back my tears
   i've counted the years

that You've not known my pain
   in the night
   left and right
   in the day
   any Word You say
   will linger
   in my mind
   throughout time
   in the way
   of any of my truths
   that may
   become a singer

The Winds of Mankind

and then, there was light...

echoes of mankind blew to Him
like wind from everest

did He hear it?
their love and agony
their sins and secrets
their prayers and denouncements of faith
their loss of land and gain of power
their castles in the sand and their final hour...

or was it just the wind?

Grief Waters

bagged head
   forced to walk
   weak
   starving for love
   expression
   freedom.

barefoot
   i feel the soft sand
   pleasant, at least
   familiarity is present, at least.

they stop me
   they break the chains that bond me
   they remove the bag.

i wondered why i felt no ocean breeze
   only sun beams.

the ocean is dead
   i've been brought here to revive it
   forcibly.

i ask how
    they say my grief
    it's inside
    and i won't let it out
    until now
    until i'm forced to.

who the fuck do you think i am?

i'm the uprooter
    the rain taker
    lightning thief
    the pain maker
    joy raker
    soul shaker
    the heartbreaker
    missing crust of the earth
    the guilt layer
    the earthquaker.

i am not the creator of the ocean
    but damn i wish i had been the one who killed it.

they say "we know you are not the creator of the ocean
    but we also know you are not the creator of grief
    yet you have it for some reason.

first as small as a grain of salt
    then layers of onions
        equal to the pounds you weighed from the womb of your mother
        the tons of it that came with language

GRIEF WATERS

how a kept word could hurt inside
how the last conversation with a loved one could forbid you to cry
to the megaton weight of wanting to die.

you haven't fooled anyone
   not even yourself
   not even us."

i've been distracted
   delusional
   and i knew this wasn't usual.

this is fucking stupid.

i don't cry in front of anyone
   not even God has seen my tears in recent years
   where is the big Man i should still fear?
   is He still covered in His Sons tears?
   is He even here?
   He's controlled my life and i've YET to see His face
   He is grotesque!
   HOW MANY OF MY PRAYERS WILL KEEP PENDING
   UPON HIS GOLDEN DESK?

a crisp SNAP
   a lever came down
   pulled – the sun swapped places
   as the moon shot over the land.

i forgot about her
   she shined on me

pulled me in close but i soon moved on my own accord
right to that old shore.

who?
   who will answer my call?
   is it you, dear God, behind the moon?
   mother nature?
   mother?
   father?
   brother?
   sister?
   friend?
   foe?
   teacher?
   lover?
   stranger?

what is this creeping sensation?
   this lump in my throat
   this pounding in my hollowed out chest?

i thought no one was home
   i thought
   i… was not home
   in my own body

i thought
   for years
   i was lost
   for years
   i could not find him

   even though i am him
   i am the man in the mirror
   have i been revealed?

all of you have seen me
   for who i am?
   at my lowest?
   at my worst?
   my family
   my friends
   from the old faces
   to the new
   i have always been naked
   God asks
   WHO TOLD YOU THAT?
   i tell Him…

i saw it
   at blue night
   in the reflection of the river
   i saw myself
   and i was terrified
   because darkness surrounded me
   my chest appeared stiff and still
   and i couldn't tell if it was moving

so i put on masks
   i buried things
   everything
   the child inside
   the man down the road

to make my chest bigger
i put people in light places
in hopes the dark part of myself wouldn't find them
and they could reflect the light i forgot within
through my blood and bones
a skeleton of what i could be

i burned things
   in an attempt to feel something
   anything

i put on clothes
   so at least that way
   i could see if the fabric moved
   i could see if my heart pumped
   i could see if i was breathing in the reflection
   because i wasn't sure
   if i was a zombie
   or if
   i
   was
   living...

a rumble
   a distant, liberating rumble
   rushing through my body
   bursting through my heart —
   is this what you felt
   dear earth
   when God first quenched your thirst?
   did He give you tears?

GRIEF WATERS

and now you proudly show them

come, oh great Luna
   pull the weeping from within me
   just as you pull the tides
   extract my horrors and guilt
   all that i have buried
   for what i thought
   was safekeeping and untouched secrets
   was in fact feeding the lion

reap the seeds i have sown
   grab the lion by its mane
   and yank it out of me
   make my skin separate from suicidal temptation
   from self-destruction
   and drown,
   not me,
   but those horrible thoughts
   down into your eternal abyss
   never to see the light of day
   never to breathe in my flesh

pull my heart out into the white, night sky
   show me that it is beating
   show me that i am alive
   wring out the impostor
   tell me why the word forgiveness
   was planted in my dreams
   twenty years in time
   that word has surrounded me

yelling to the past
   yelling to the future
   all this time
   i had the key
   to live or die

oh Luna,
   let my tears show you how long i have suffered
   how long i have wanted
   not to die
   but to live
   ...
   tears burst from my eyes like fire from Mt. Helen
   like rain that falls from Heaven
   like God working 6 days
   to rest, He just needed that lucky number seven
   ...
   before i knew it
   the water of my grief
   washed my feet.

The Great Brown Heron & The Bronze Woman

on my back
    warm sand underneath me
    the sun rays
    they burn over the dunes
    blazing
    scraping upon the earth
    the blue sky
    clear as crystal waters
    something i am
    in dire
    need
    of

a sound softly lands on my ears
    what is that machine?
    that instrument
    miles away, it echoes
    a trumpet
    a symphony of Eden
    the ground jolts once
    i thought myself dead and alone here

but alas, i sense an energy
  a great brown heron soars above
  i crawl
  shuffle
  to my
  feet

this desert is vast but i cannot see
  the dunes block my vision of anything else
  the heron has disappeared over
  i approach the dune
  beast-like – i crawl up
  until i plant myself
  atop the dune
  like a
  flag

i see the great brown heron
  perched on a stone fountain
  the water trickles down into the basin
  a bronze woman sits
  washing her hands slowly
  the heron unbothered
  and not
  bothering
  her

the land is flat up here
  there is a sea of sand
  to the far left of the fountain
  where a cliff dips hundreds of feet

THE GREAT BROWN HERON & THE BRONZE WOMAN

    i approach the fountain
    dying of thirst
    like an unquenched spirit
    like a
    wild
    dog

i stumble to the fountain
    dropping to my knees
    i dunk my head in entirely
    the water touching my shoulders
    the heron slightly turns its head to me
    the woman keeps washing her hands
    i've been under for half a minute
    two minutes
    three hundred
    and sixty
    seconds

the bronze woman stands and pulls me out
    by the collar of my tattered shirt
    yanked from the fountain
    quick to catch my breath
    i was so consumed
    so deeply entrenched
    into the dna of the water
    the pull of it
    the amassing
    weight

"what did you see?" asks the bronze woman

was that him?
"i asked a question"
and i need answers
was that him??
is it
Him?

in the water of the fountain
   before she yanked me out
   i saw a bronze man in the reflection
   long, black, wool-like hair
   battered and unkempt
   a crown of thorns upon Him
   staring at
   me

i free myself from her grasp of my collar
   i am face to face with the water
   i splash my hands in
   ripples break the surface
   but He wavers not
   i tell Him

become a man again
   trade with me
   become me, Jesus of Nazareth (please)

tell me i'm a sinner
   when You run between and to
   the corners of my mind
   resist everything

    even before
    you arrive
    at the
    mountain

His reflection begins
    to
    fade

lead me out of this desert
    take me back
    why'd You lead me here?
    hey!
    take me to heaven!
    or take me back! (He is gone)
    why'd you leave me here??
    TAKE ME
    OR TAKE ME BACK!

the great brown heron turns its gaze across the sea of sand
    to a cliff-side city
    small in our vision
    close enough to see figures
    few moving things
    wooden objects
    in the center up a path
    to the cliff
    metal shining
    from the
    rays of
    sun

"when did He allow them to start making demands?"
   asks the bronze woman to the heron
     "i have no idea... but it's about to reset" says the heron
     the bronze woman sits back down
     on the edge of the fountain
     just like before
     gently washing her hands

the ground jolts
   the water in the fountain vibrates
   that sound rests on my ears again
   carried by the wind
   the symphony of Eden
   carried with it – noises of what seems to be
   an angry crowd
   i get up from the fountain
   turning my head to the distance
   across the sea of sand
   to that distant city
   by the
   cliff-side

what's all the commotion over there?
   did the heron just speak?
   or is
   someone else
   here?

"what did you see?" asks the bronze woman
   did you not hear me?
     "does the wind pass through

that big hollow head of yours
in one ear and out the other?
is there no fishing net
that catches words
like salmon
for your mind to digest it
after it's been looked over
flayed
deboned
seasoned and seared?"

are you trying to mock me?
   "trying?"
watch your tongue
"no, it is you who need watch yours"
she keeps washing – never looking at me
"i birthed this world and nurtured
the tongue of man until the flood
you are a byproduct of babel
i am embedded with the first language
the mere first words of the earth
the third being
in His image.

i am your involuntary mother of mankind
   your autonomy and free will
   your life and death
   and don't you forget it."

"he thinks himself complex" says the great brown heron
   "but deep down he is simple"

says the heron.
"says man... my duality differs from yours"
how so?
"first to truly live
and first to regret.
made alive without a mother."
they don't look at me
they keep their eyes on the crowd
moving up the
cliff-side
city

"yours – war and peace"
   it's not that simple
   "oh, but it is
   it is a scale of sand and mountain stone
   peace has to pour in gently
   a fluid motion
   after the weight of war
   is spurned away"

i move away from the fountain
   pacing back and forth angrily
   and i stop
   glaring at them both
   my back to the city

the ground jolts
   i almost lose my footing
   that instrument
   no, that orchestra

THE GREAT BROWN HERON & THE BRONZE WOMAN

finding my ears again
that symphony of Eden
what does it mean?
i turn around and
the crowd is
gone

"what did you see?" asks the bronze woman
my life in its entirety
"right… move along then"
what?
that's it?
i can't even speak to Him?

"He's busy" says the heron
what a grand excuse
"do you believe it?" asks the bronze woman
what?
"look over there – across the way
where our eyes are set
across the
sea of
sand"

i fix my eyes across to the city
a crowd of people flock like chickens
moving up the path
to the cliff-side
gradually
few people in the center
i cannot see them clearly

but they carry something wooden
closer to them
people with shimmering
metal

what could possibly be shining like that?
"roman soldiers" says the heron
what?
in armor?
where am i?
what year is it?
am i
dreaming?

who are those people surrounding?
who is
in the
center?

"would you believe me?" asks the bronze woman
"would you then be able
to see the objects
that are
being
carried?"

"your war and peace" says the heron
"it's internal and external
don't think for a second
you would want it any other way.
i didn't know it

    my time
    being a
    man

i could not see beyond my heart
    and so i beseeched Him years ago
    before everything changed
    before everyone became
    to help me
    seek
    revenge

i know that it is His
    but He gave way to it anyways
    so i immediately sought it.
    if it was another human
    i would've done it before cain
    but now what you see of me
    is my regret and rage manifested
    the first hunter

BEHOLD
    THE GREAT BROWN HERON
    FOR I BLOODIED
    AND SLEW
    THE SNAKE

…and it did nothing"

the ground jolts
    this time i steady myself as it rumbles

then i see it
i see the crowd disappear
before they reach the cliff
like none of it ever happened
all the while
on my ears
the symphony of
Eden

"do you believe?" asks the bronze woman
   whom is still gently washing
   i don't know what i believe
   "then he is merely a man who once existed
   and nothing more"
   how can you say that?
   "is something incorrect?"
   no- well, yes... maybe
   "so informative... what have you ever been sure of?"
   that... that i was alive
   "are you truly sure of that?"
   i know i was alive
   "how do you know?"

i just watched it all
   "ah, you watched it" says the bronze woman
   "now go live it"
   what?
   "this is your free will
   go do what you please with it"
   but i was so hurt
   the world was on fire

love and hate rivaled to a bitter end
i lost so many things
so many people
i lost
myself

is there no hope left?
   "there is always hope" says the brown heron
   what about him? in the center of the crowd?
   "are you not worried about the other two alongside the man?"
   i... i do not know them
   "but suddenly you know the man in the middle?
   it is a gesture for you take -
   his actions
   look, there they are now"

it starts again
   i see them
   moving up along the path
   surrounded by roman soldiers
   carrying wooden objects
   followed by an angry crowd
   we hear all this
   the winds of mad men
   repeating their detests over and over
   in the same shape
   but a different voice every time
   and suddenly
   the cry of a woman
   breaking through the anger

"take the gesture – whether you believe or not" says the great brown heron
    i watch one last time
    the men move towards the cliff-side
    the man in the center struggles
    stopping
    for what seems like a deadly moment
    and he is moving again
    as is the orchestra's instruments
    that symphony of Eden
    landing on my ears

i turn and walk away from the fountain
    but a question burns inside of me
    i look back to the great brown heron and the bronze woman
    and i ask
    what does the gesture mean?

"love harder."

SOULPUNK: PART TWO

i suffocated
wanted endless night
took time – contemplated
look at where i'm at now
i want my life

...

i am
breathing
feeling
living

...

i am
breathing
feeling
living

Bone Man In The Rays

i dropped your husk in an open field
    and danced as the skeleton i am, in the sun
    for a moment i was reminded of your flesh

your depression
    was self-cannibalism
    cells trying to grow against nihilism

the wind whispered against my ribs
    and i wondered if Adam and Eve
    ever questioned which one of them were incomplete

the grass stained my bones green
    as it did you in your youth
    when it would streak against your light blue jeans

a dog trotted up to me
    demanding a bone
    for him to own

can you not see that i am dancing?
    "where is your heart?"

BONE MAN IN THE RAYS

i cannot remember which house it is in

"would it not be in the house of the living?"
   i do not believe they do such things in there
   "how could you even dare?"

"go get your bloody, beating heart
   you're a skeleton dancing in the sun
   but your flesh is not yet done"

i am breaking free from humanity
   from God and destiny
   i did not know the boy before the growth spurt
   and i never did know the man in the mirror

"must i remind you of my teeth?
   you are not supposed to be here
   i am the reapers dog
   and you should not be this close to death
   by your own choosing"

"you know the boy and the man
   the bones you hold together are theirs
   you just wish to burn off their pains
   and keep their happiness for yourself
   but that is not your job"

no? then *what* is, dog?
   "to hold them together
   when the weight of living gets heavy
   and to make their flesh dance

making life sweet and heady"

Fear & Valor (A Letter)

dear sean,

you've been here as long as time has known you.
   the park bench the sun
   God
   the pain the wonder the fear
   the wars the passion the love
   the hate the questions of purpose
   the skin the art
   fate

time must end somewhere
   do you remember? it feels like forever
   a time i could not find for us.

because hell is going to find you
   trap you
   hurt you
   trick you
   all just to punish you for being here
   walking on earth.

i have been the bearer of bad news for you throughout time
　　because i am you
　　　　and i am going to climb us out of hell.

Breathe

in the wild
   the high tide fire
   the animals scurry away
   'cause i'm hurryin' their way

i burned down that old family home
   twisted voices on the flip phones
   pictures that captured peace like marble stone
   food that buried grief with greens & chicken bones

maybe if i breathe now
   that young kid'll calm down
   maybe if i breathe now
   that young kid'll calm down

i pray for the rain
   to dowse my flames
   the anger that lives in my past
   such a worrisome, plagued path

manipulating my memories
   manipulating my emotions today

    the past and present energies
    leadin' my future astray

maybe if i breathe now
    that young kid'll calm down
    maybe if i breathe now
    that young kid'll calm down

1940

i wonder what you thought when you first met me.
   the last son of one of your eight children.
   wonder what you saw when you first held me.
   the youngest, at the time, of your grandchildren.
   my mind was too young to recall when i first talked to you.
   i know that we bonded well.
   the dandelions that i gave you and my mother are now a tattoo.
   it healed well.
   i remember you before you lost your memory.
   before you lost me.
   it wasn't the disease that erased us,
   nor your declining health,
   it was my fear of you forgetting me.
   i didn't reach out anymore until your last two weeks on earth.
   your voice- your soul, reached out to answer three of my questions,
   similar to how your hands reached out to hold me after my birth.
   on these sands, i cried for you in solitude.
   a cry i haven't felt since i was a child.
   in my heart you told me it was okay.
   and i found it in me to forgive that child.
   i can't explain the spirituality of it.
   i felt your presence so deep i kept looking for your foot steps in the

sand
   trying to comprehend some of it.
   you found peace.
   God gave that to you.
   i prayed that for you.
   by the water i released my guilt.
   i was reminded of your grace by the beauty of the sun.
   how it hugged the water,
   no matter how cold it got.
   how it reached for the water,
   no matter how low it got.
   how it was there for the water,
   no matter how indifferent it got.
   how it breathed on the water,
   no matter how lonely it got.
   the pain was so rich that i smiled for a moment when i cried.
   happy, finally, after almost 3 years, that for you, i cried.

on these sands
   i had to process your long absence
   on these sands
   i had to accept your death
   otherwise i would be dooming myself to wallow in this pain and guilt
   the pain that was so real
   it kept you and the shame alive for me in my heart.

i know you would not want such a burden on my soul
   because to release you is not to let you go
   but to love you truthfully
   honestly

1940

as you once were
and as you are now
a resident of heaven
and to allow myself to heal
instead of burying grief with distractions and vices
and so, i let my tears join the ocean before me.

...

when i was very young,
    when you still had that green house in glen burnie,
    you and i were fixing to plant a tomato garden
in the spring.
but i had dug too deep,
and when the rain came,
it flooded and ruined the ground.

the next time i came back,
    you had fixed it all
    and the vines were growing.

you had fixed my mistake,
    one i thought was absolute.
    and now i'm old enough
    to fix my own.

If I Knew The Words Back Then

i have given my characters nearly half of my grief
   i have drowned them in my sorrows and self-pity...

the other half of grief i have reserved for myself
   is squeezed from the fruits of life
   hearing my parents laughter
   knowing what will become of them the older i get
   to love my brothers child
   knowing what has become of our relationship
   building love for years
   and having it crumble in under a minute

the ignorance i harbored in adolescence
   was a belief that the 'me' that desired to not be alive -
   was demonic.
   an unfortunate pitfall that grew in the back of my mind
   from churches and cultural stigmatization
   but the fact of my life is that he was not a demon.
   he was the part of me i could not understand
   and the part i could not heal from depression
   from trauma
   from my own sludge of hate

IF I KNEW THE WORDS BACK THEN

    bitterness
    guilt
    anger and
    silence —
    the part i could not treat on the inside.

i could not see with unburdened eyes
    and how could i?
    i grew up wanting to harm no one
    yet i learned harm from the world and repeated it loud and quietly.

hate disguised itself as 'i feel, therefore, i am alive'
    it burrowed and nested underneath my young, impressionable heart
    slow cooking my desire to actually live
    free from what my eyes saw
    free from what my body felt
    it took life and turned it into something i resented

but
    in the same breath
    forgiveness came to me as a word in a dream
    before it meant anything true to me.

the day i took a step towards becoming a man
    was the day i forgave myself for letting my grandmother go
    while she was still alive.
    her memory, body, laughter - roadblocked by dementia.
    she had forgotten my face the last time i saw her at 17 years old.
    that feeling,
    looking her in the eyes and realizing she couldn't see me, but a random boy,

was locked away for years.

six years later from that moment
    and two years later after her passing
    i found myself grieving on an empty beach.
    a week long trip that a commercial paid for.
    the waves of emotion within would have drowned many goliaths;
    the deepest sorrow was apologizing when she couldn't hear it
    because living in a world of praise, who was going to validate my grief
    if she couldn't?
    such thoughts
    my untimely misunderstanding of the power of the tongue
    and unchallenged beliefs.

i followed up my apologies to her by forgiving myself,
    fear stood in the way of me loving her properly.
    i understood she would forget;
    i did not understand she would forget **me**.

so i sat
    tears running
    tears drying
    forgiving myself a thousand and one times until that ignorant, adolescent 'me' heard it
    and until he forgave himself for being too frightened of the unknown to love.

for ignorance was bliss for him,
    but it was cruel for me.
    and in that forgiveness for myself, to myself, by myself,

IF I KNEW THE WORDS BACK THEN

i understood the power of forgiveness comes from love.

and if that would be true,
   then i am a witness of love.
   and i have acted upon love more than upon hate,
   not because i do not hate death,
   but because she is loved; surviving in my mind.

time has showed me time and time again who i am, what i am,
   where i am, how i am, why i am
   time does not move away from us,
   time slows down to guide the worlds revolutions
   and since mankind has existed
   the revolution has been love
   but trust, it is a hard, deafening, uphill battle.

i found
   that the acts of love
   are so grand and small
   choosing to cook for someone
   in their most dreadful of moments
   i imagine, could impact the heart & soul
   as much as the Godly act of splitting fish and bread
   or simply letting them know
   they are not alone in their sorrows.

i often wonder if my friends understand
   how much the love they've poured into my hand
   impacted my survival
   and vice versa.

just as much as they impact me,
   so does my aunt in new york
   who sends me Gods Word
   from pastors and preachers she trusts —
something i struggle to find.

i've had to step back
   and realize life need not be grand all the time
   for there to be meaning or purpose;
   expecting it to be such has brought me great suffering.
   for there is something to be said
   about repetition, normalcy, the mundane—
   about stillness and rest.
   how else would one get the big picture
   they strive to achieve
   without going through everyday life?
   i have learned the hard way
   you cannot cheat experience.
   no matter the reward or pain
   why would i want to anymore?

it would be on par with copy and paste
   and that sounds like the death of perspective and individuality.

in the midst of the mist,
   i find myself disappearing into a fantasy.
   escaping reality by driving deep within
   to bestow love upon those very same broken characters
   i spoke of at the start,
   only in hopes to find some answer that maybe the God i believe in
placed there.

IF I KNEW THE WORDS BACK THEN

is there a purpose,
    a destiny,
    a path,
    a fate?
    if there is true love, is there also true hate?

if so
    the scale must always lean towards love
    because love is in the living.
    otherwise you risk losing sight,
    you risk becoming a zombie,
    walking, but not retaining,
    watching, but not experiencing,
    breathing, but not living
    death before death.

the easy part is letting go to hate
    the hard part is holding on to love

if i can love you
    for one day
    even for just one moment
    i hope that is all it takes for you to **remain alive**.

Senses

that chill autumn air
   bird chirping, gray morning flare
   cold rubber of my old cars spare
   the rustling of fingers gliding through coarse hair

the fabric of simplicity
   bundled up safely
   life's present to us
   an easy nudge towards our senses

hands glide across bedsheets
   knew it was morning by the sounds of nature
   hugging so closely – i almost forgot your scent
   had my eyes noticed the wrinkles on your hands?
   too busy for a home cooked meal

the fabric
   a layer of warmth
   oh, what a warm meal does for the body
   what a sweet smell does for the body
   what a soft tune does for the body
   what a hot shower does for the body

SENSES

and as i wipe the steamy mirror
i take notice...
what a handsome somebody

Ten Years To Send You On Your Way

you've gone away
   but i can't escape
   your face
   in night
   and day
   when i burn awake
   you've left a hole
   a gape
   a sound
   a scrape
   you make
   i found the line
   the rope today
   so i grabbed my end
   and cut away
   drifting down the fog
   i watch you fade
   a way
   you've never gone before.

Au Revoir Raven

ten years ago
   just kids, you and i
   fourteen and fifteen
   "poetry is a lost art
   but you definitely found it"

that's what you told me
   but by that time, you had already left
   home-schooled for a couple years
   only saw you once in between that time
   after a talent show i did
   then you disappeared

i wouldn't have gone deeper
   had it not been for you
   sharing poems in gym class
   then online 'til you were gone

and suddenly, you popped back up
   after high school
   you'd eloped and wanted me to be a witness
   for your courthouse marriage

then you were gone again
   still the same girl i knew
   but different plans for the both of us
   no more moving into a warehouse
   or loft
   in san francisco

then, you were back again
   covid was a rough one
   maybe it scared me into seeing you again
   because i reached out – and you said yes

you were the same
   but a woman now
   married in day
   a woman of the night

the world got bigger
   and you adapted
   you went deeper
   deeper into life
   love affection art
   womanhood beauty discovery

you showed me
   from early on
   there's courage in living in all your truths
   but oftentimes i muffled such singers out of fear

and so it took me awhile
   to go deeper

i didn't know myself
having moved around so much
i was never quite sure if it was okay
to truly start living again

because
    by God, i was alive when i was a kid
    and it seemed when everything felt right
    i started 'living'
    i was there for a lot of it
    but i was so confused
    so in denial
    scatter brained
    i tried to find a crutch for love
    everywhere i turned
    to every girl i knew
    because if she was beautiful
    she was game

i loved hard
    not because i was passionate
    or because any of it was real
    but because i felt something was missing
    and i needed that same love to be returned
    and every time it wasn't
    i was devastated angry wounded
    upside down
    right was left and left was right
    inverted heart
    self harming

nowadays
    life is revealing itself and i focus on myself
    because the love i so desperately wanted to give
    is no longer desperate
    yet, platonically it is alive and well
    and romantically, it is in a gentle hibernation
    a cocoon
    transforming into something safer
    richer fuller honest
    non-smothering
    as i grow in age and emotional intelligence —
    an unselfish love.

i am living
    but
    i was
    all this time
    even back then with all the pains and poems
    even when it was just us in gym

i wrote a letter
    had it with me the last time we met
    i never knew if you did marry
    until you mentioned your husband that day
    you asked me why i wanted to see you
    needed, to see you
    that you had somewhere to be with him
    i had that letter on my lap
    and then
    i stuffed it in my pocket

AU REVOIR RAVEN

you'll never know what that letter said
   hell, i don't even remember what it said
   i had to let go of the anxious fear i had for your life
   knowing what profession you were getting into at night
   but you've always been able to handle yourself
   and i've grown to respect your silence

you were one of the first people
   to treat me well when i came to california
   and your rapture from my life that early
   gave me an agony i hadn't known before.

i have finally learned to speak in truth
   and thus, being in a family of lecturers
   for the betterment of myself
   i have always listened to you
   whenever your voice found my ears
   my dear raven.

but now i accept
   that such a sound for me
   shall be nevermore.

And She Whispered To Me "It's Okay To Live"

you
    carved out marble
    angel to marvel
    resting so artful
    never to startle

you
    could take my rib
    my breath is yours
    could take my lips
    my words are yours

you
    kiss goodbye to the sun
    pull in the moon
    tilt the love til it runs
    a taste of silver spoon

you
    sweet embrace of warmth
    remind me i'm standin' right here

AND SHE WHISPERED TO ME "IT'S OKAY TO LIVE"

    if wings could adorn
    you would grace the room right here

you
    liberate my heart
    remindin' me it's okay to live (without you)
    liberate my heart
    remind me it's okay to live (without you)

Dognation

it should be noted
that the west
practices their most damning atrocities
always abroad

but a citizen must know
the dog never forgets
how to turn its fangs
against its own tail

November 5th, 2024

i'm not sure i ever recognized the stripes
   as my own
   flapping
   gnashing in the wind like a blood hurricane
   blue and white convinces you it touches the sky
   but man has put it there with the red of others
   and man has made it clear
   his nature is dominion
   his God is no longer in heaven
   but in he who sits upon the white throne.

i have hope that things will change
   but peace
   is gathered after the storm

when humanity ultimately decides
   to resuscitate
   rather than inflict pain

when the powers that be
   become lifeboats
   rather than dreadnoughts.

and until those moments come
   the power of change
   is up to the singers of truth.

Same Divine Word

simply put —
　i am conflicted

i pray to the same God they call upon to strike down the innocent
　the same God they call upon to help them snatch people off the streets
　the same God i call upon to help me get this new job
　the same God they call upon to wash them of the blood of those they hate
　the same God i call upon to wash me of my sins
　the same God they call upon to deliver them safely through the valley
　the same God they call upon to bless and elect a rapist
　the same God i call upon to help with the rent this month
　the same God they praise after putting kids in cages
　the same God a palestinian child pleads with for her life
　the same God an african woman pleads with for her country
　the same God the atheist calls upon when there's nowhere left to run
　the same God the prisoner calls upon day and night for forgiveness
　the same God the warden calls upon to bless his baton
　the same God that will apparently judge them all

SOULPUNK

the same God that will judge me

mans dogma
   or mans dog-like nature?

free will is a mothafucka, ain't it?

To Whom The Light Touches

what was done in the dark,
   has been brought to light

and the perpetrators don't think they've perpetrated
   and the colonizers believe they are freedom fighters
   and the trespassers believe they have been trespassed against
   and the world powers believe they are on defense
   and the greedy believe they have nothing
   and the extremists swear they've lost something

and the politicians have used you as stepping stools
   and the corporations have bent and looped around rules
   and the racist has become blind to apartheid
   and the impulsive blind to foresight

and somehow, even in the dark,
   children have been separated by color, ethnicity & border
   and they've been slain & enslaved wickedly

but the powers that be shouted at us in the dark
   exclaiming it is all for tranquility

do they not understand
    their bombs have created the light in which we see their faces
    their hatred has spread fire in which we see the path of chaos
    but yet,
    love screams out - because **it must**
    and it is the saving grace of our existence

A Divided House Will Fall

nature gave enough
   man chipped away
   on this side of the highway

public housing
   barred corner stores
   broken sidewalks
   cop hot spots
   parks with needles
   and dirty bathrooms
   uniform schools
   with metal detectors
   check cashing
   and loan lending
   shoulder to shoulder
   with gas stations
   a pharmacy
   across the street
   from two liquor stores
   and coin laundry
   a busted fire hydrant
   turned into

a street kiddie pool
adjacent to the corner
where cop cars linger
waiting to push the homeless
further down the block

nature gave enough
  man chipped away
  on that side of the highway

neighborhood pool
  street sweepers
  banks
  gated houses
  twenty four hour gym
  stadiums
  skin care
  and real estate
  billboards
  healthier grocery stores
  no rust
  on the park slide
  or in the bathroom
  tracks
  just for walking
  jogging
  skating
  neighborhood watch signs
  bike lanes
  car charging stations
  no ebt signs

A DIVIDED HOUSE WILL FALL

   in the windows
   schools known nationally
   fancier
   well-off

the naive
   and the architects
   will tell you
   it's coincidence
   a coin toss
   happenstance
   no one planned this
   don't be ridiculous
   an absurdist
   conspiracy theorist

how could a highway divide a people?
   you marched for this

is it **you,** now?
   thought it was **we**…

ah, i don't know
   maybe i am
   just trippin'

but still
   i wonder
     …

Diner (Table For 1 Broke Man)

almost midnight
   sittin' at a diner
   waitin' on my paycheck
   told the waitress it'd be a while 'til i order
   got a water
   though, the glass ain't rinsed enough
   it's squeaky clean
   but too fresh of a glass
   i can taste the soap in every sip
   momma always threatened my brother
   told him she'd rinse his mouth with soap
   i guess the fuckin' sin has fallen on me
   it's funny

i used to come here a lot
   years ago
   order somethin' for myself
   or maybe a girl i liked
   if i was lucky that day
   let alone that year
   and still walk away with a few dollars
   well i got two dollars and some change

DINER (TABLE FOR 1 BROKE MAN)

i can't get shit today
inflation takin' my last hopes
that even when it's hot it rains on me
it's funny

i told myself not to write about it
   but there's an american flag in the window
   staring at me as i judge our economy
   or myself for poor fiscal responsi—yeah, yeah
   well i'm still waiting for my money
   now if only i knew how to correctly use the word irony
   this shit might be funny

don't take the cursing for anger
   i'm pretty relaxed
   only thing that'll make me wanna flip a table in this bitch
   is my check hittin' after it's been taxed
   but, hell, it could always be worse
   instead of my taxes feeding kids in schools
   it could go to bombing kids in their sleep
   "at least they're getting something" - u.s. government, probably

maybe i should've stayed in school
   or took up some soul-sucking job in ai creation
   bet i could pay for a burger and fries right now
   but i get sick thinking about one thing
   how many of my graduated friends payin' off debts now?
   took a sip of my soapy ass water
   rememberin'
   shit, i'm twenty five with small debts now

what is it with the united states and our diners?
   is it the coffee past midnight?
   the conversations under loud music?
   the nostalgia of good and cheap food?
   it ain't that anymore, i'll tell ya
   can't be the soapy ass water, either
   maybe it's the clinking of plates and cutlery
   a noise reminding you that you aren't alone

somebody's in the booth next to you
   thinking about how much they should tip, too
   thinking about what they'd do
   if they were a rich fool
   or taking in the family time
   with stuffed bellies wondering if they should finish
   this good, unhealthy food
   it ain't all too bad
   that's the funny thing about america
   you could be having a shitty night
   and realize you're lucky enough to laugh about it
   'cause it could always get worse

and yet
   right now
   it ain't
   it is just what it is
   and i should not be mad at that
   i cannot be mad at that
   cause i walked an hour to get here
   built a little sweat
   and they ain't chargin' me for water…

DINER (TABLE FOR 1 BROKE MAN)

at least not yet.

Black American Ambiance

there is a weird happiness dawning on america
   one i could possibly trust if i were more unconscious
   yet i hear the blues in the back of my mind
   drums, saxophones, keys
   speaking things my soul cannot form into words
   the rhythm that keeps my cerebellum flowing
   keeping my body moving, not ever in just one state

how does coltrane know my struggles?
   and armstrong, too?
   i catch a city bus, a plane, a train
   i'd take anything to escape the pain

blue like the sky spies me
   everyday anything can remind me of the disdain
   america has had for me and my family
   and everyday i have to make a decision not to revisit such distaste
   but i must also not attempt to cleanse the palette
   for that would be absolving america of its sins
   and i am afraid that is too much blood for any man
   yes, any Man

BLACK AMERICAN AMBIANCE

i have to choose freedom
   i have to choose curiosity
   i have to choose the might of black joy
   i have to choose a love that touches animosity
   not a personal love, but a love for the country
   because i have to be somewhat mad to love america
   for what it really is
   not what martin dreamed it could be

i often wonder if he discussed the burning house
   with Jesus
   after all, they've both been to the mountaintop
   the only difference is, when martin got there
   america hid its future evils

but i believe he knew there was always going to be
   more work that needed to be done
   he and those who walked in line before me
   so who am i to get out of line,
   losing my place,
   because i'd rather be content with what it is now?
   i've eaten with the very tongue that speaks out against the red, white, and blue
   against false statutes and statues
   the same palette as america for so long now
   sipping away on a bad batch of black coffee
   questioning if it's a good thing
   that i could ever become accustomed to

Bags Packed

across the street
    a beautiful black woman smiling

she's 'laxed at the bus stop,
    both arms stretched, chillin' over the bench.
    bags packed.

ready to go,
    tackle the world,
    or just to go home.

can't hear her giggles,
    but i can damn sure feel 'em.
    turned my bad mood into a good one,
    black woman sure do know how to heal 'em.

cigarette in hand,
    she don't pay no mind.
    alone without a man,
    she ain't got the time.

bags packed,

BAGS PACKED

    ready to go,
    tackle the world,
    or just to go home.

i can hear her sigh,
    across all the traffic.
    hope her life's a good time,
    but i'm sure she knows the word tragic.

look down and you could miss her,
    she want someone to look up with through the pain.
    a stranger: for some reason i now miss her,
    cause she's gone now that her bus came.

her bags were packed,
    she was ready to go,
    tackling the world,
    or just ready to go home.

but i wonder
    what is that third thing
    dear beautiful black woman?

By The Curb

claire de lune plays on the piano
   as the chair i push them in
   rumbles over the bumps
   in the main lobby

purple, black, green
   gray, teal, and other
   scrub color schemes
   flocks of red & blue littered with fresh, studious faces

i wheel them out to the entrance
   softly pushing the brake
   and i stand beside them
   as we await their ride in heat or cold
   night or day

by the curb
   i have heard the words

"don't get married"
   as he waits for his wife

BY THE CURB

"my family and i don't talk anymore"
   as she waits for her boyfriend

"make sure you put money away for retirement"
   as she waits for her husband

"did you serve?"
   as the wording and symbol on his hat says *vietnam veteran*

"can't wait to finally be in my own bed again"
   as she holds her three day old baby

"i'm afraid… please don't hurt me"
   as her son and i
   gently help her in the car
   i could not look away from her lost eyes
   something reminding me of my grandmother's mind

"find your path in life and stick to it,
   and if one path closes, find another"
   as he waits for his son

"i'm 82 years old with lung cancer and i'm here visiting my younger sister"
   as she's about to drive herself home

i sat with another woman for a while
   her people came down to the front with her
   but they left to go get the car

i asked

those your siblings, or friends, or?
"friends, yeah. we've been friends for over 40 years."
oh wow, that's lovely.
"yeah… we just actually lost a friend two weeks ago to cancer."
oh, i'm sorry to hear that.
"thank you…
death is… not good."
no, it is not.
"and i'm sure you've experienced it, too."
yeah…

by the curb
   i have heard the words,
   the breath,
   the want
   for life to persist
   and to put to bed
   long wishes,
   and long regrets.

Sandcastles

what is capable of such a soft thing?
   dreams of kings and queens?

i pity those people
   who kick down their castles
   trading the sand for a window
   that which they stare out of for eternity
   like a curse
   never to have thrill from their dreams
   but only from the survival of life

don't build your dreams on stone
   the freedom of the sand is everything
   you can start again
   be anything again
   demolish and create
   watch as they manifest differently
   and become one in the same

the mountain stone cannot follow you home
   but the sand can

The People's Cocktail

recipe for 2+ people
    if more than 2, add half part and taste before serving
    and i know it's a lot of ingredients
    just put away your mathematician hat for now

here we go —

2 people
    1 part topic
    2 parts genuine
    2 parts feeling
    1 part location
    half part music (can do without)
    2 slices of life
    1 part day or night

for extra depth
    add 1 part revelation
    2 parts reminiscing
    2 parts closure
    2 parts love

THE PEOPLE'S COCKTAIL

for relaxation, 2 parts platonic
  for spice, 2 parts longing

What's New, Friends?

we've got new jobs
   we've got new hobbies
   we've got new tattoos
   we've got new lobbies

we've got new partners
   we've got new cars
   we've got new passports
   we've got new bars

we've got new problems
   we've got new places
   we've got new drinks
   we've got new faces

we've got new classes
   we've got new foods
   we've got new vices
   we've got new moods

we've got new prayers
   we've got new wines

WHAT'S NEW, FRIENDS?

we've got new churches
we've got new lines

we've got new travels
we've got new monies
we've got new secrets
we've got new honeys

we've got new clothes
we've got new beds
we've got new couches
we've got new steads

we've got new grudges
we've got new dogs
we've got new goodbyes
we've got new cogs

we've got new plans
we've got new tears
we've got new debts
we've got new years

we've got new doctors
we've got new weddings
we've got new insurances
we've got new beddings

we've got new funerals
we've got new gyms
we've got new sobrieties

    we've got new rims

we've got new kids
    we've got new miles
    we've got new albums
    we've got new riles

we've got new degrees
    we've got new hearts
    we've got new apologies
    we've got new starts

we've got you.

Reconciliation

all i was given
all i have given
all i was not
all i have not

will only rest on my shoulders
to crush

but
if i lift
time and time again
it shall strengthen me

i push the weight up to the heavens
all throughout time
and it will become a familiar battle
one i've defeated before

Man Standing

pushed out of the womb
   out of the arms of my mother
   and at some point or another
   i learned to stand
   walk, and run
   just to find another woman's arms to fall into

and after all the relationships
   after all the situationships
   after all the friendships
   after all the… date-ships

i understand
   my two feet have no right
   standing in front of any woman for long
   until i learn to stand
   walk, and run
   for myself

Finding Father (A Letter)

dear dad,

what a gift i have
   to look at myself
   and see parts of you

my mom was with me
   on my first day of kindergarten
   when they asked me what name i preferred
   my first name or middle
   i chose you

big rig truck
   dunking at the court
   fourth of july explosions
   an upside-down rocket
   restaurants and mall trips
   phone calls
   emails
   text messages
   money sent for christmases
   surprise pick-ups from elementary school

movies, theme parks
swooping us in rental cars
road trips in your red eighteen-wheeler
sharing the bed in the back
with either jasmine or shane
as the four of us journeyed to
new york
or pennsylvania
our common love for the birds
or my continuous venting to you
about my struggles with girls and grades in high school
years later it would be chico, california
just me and you

i'd receive a text
   from shane
   the days after you kicked them out
   telling me how i turned my back on him and jasmine
   that i stayed with you and my stepmom at the time
   for only materialistic things

cops came to the apartment
   jasmine and shane were outside already
   mom was there eventually
   christmas day or the day after
   me and shane found ourselves outside
   for just a moment
   it was only us
   he demanded i go with them
   i grew with so much anger
   turning my neck to look at him

FINDING FATHER (A LETTER)

    felt like my neck had been frozen for years
    and i was breaking it

cops asked me
    since i was old enough to decide
    what do you want to do?
    go with them
    or
    stay here?

i stayed with you
    because leaving
    would mean starting all over again

back to severn, dundalk, baltimore, maryland
    covington, kentucky brooklyn, new york
    elko, starr valley, nevada marietta, georgia
    or charleston, south carolina
    this time longer than two weeks
    or baltimore again
    maybe back in aunt vicky's basement
    after the other places fell out again
    or maybe somewhere new
    mom always wanted to live in florida

i was tired of running
    tired of moving
    tired of starting again
    torn from friends
    fear of making friends
    because i knew i'd move again

and because i never had the chance to live with you

you gave me a chance to build myself
   build myself in california without starting and stopping
   no matter what happened in that apartment
   or in the past
   or after the fact

you gave me a chance to grow
   and i wish things had worked out that way
   for my sister and brother too
   but jasmine has always been free from authority
   and shane was asked to give up his dog for you

i didn't stay because of material things

i stayed because you always said you were my father
   and if you couldn't prove it to them at the time
   you proved it to me

and in these eleven years
   of california
   for me
   we've grown
   to tell each other the truth
   to have awkward conversations
   to admit our faults and mistakes
   to depend on one another
   to be father and son

the late night phone calls

FINDING FATHER (A LETTER)

because you know i can't sleep
   or that i am working nights
   and you're often on the road early

telling each other our wishes
   or hearing the priceless joy in your voice
   when i tell you i've been cast
   in another play or film

there were long years
   when you didn't believe in that dream of mine
   but somehow God slowly changed your heart
   when you saw me onstage for the first time

i laugh reminiscing about a time in high school
   i accidentally admitted losing my virginity
   because you asked about the condoms you bought me
   and i said i only had two out of the three

but i must confess to you
   the guilt of putting my foot down against my family
   the guilt of sticking by your side
   did not whither away
   rather it took up space everyday

i held onto that longer than my brother did
   because a part of me deep inside always wanted
   to end up back in baltimore
   and i felt that urge the most
   when the freddie gray protest in 2015
   was laughed at by some new found friends in fresno

there was always a wedge between you and my mother
   and i don't know why
   maybe after this you will tell me
   maybe she will
   or maybe it is fate that i never find out

maybe it was written by God
   to show me
   that a divided house will fall
   if not mended at the pillars
   that there will always be a pot boiling
   and water spilled if no one pays attention
   that you can lose sight of love
   or realize too late that you never had it

maybe it was written by God
   to show me
   that the easy part is letting go
   but the hard part is holding on

or maybe it was just a human mistake
   and that is what allowed me to give you grace
   understanding that you are not perfect
   even though i believed it for so long

maybe that came from not seeing you
   as often as we all wish we had
   so my image of you never had time
   to truly manifest outside of my early imaginations
   and quick, fun childhood impressions
   every time you came around

FINDING FATHER (A LETTER)

    from the first moment i met you
    a smile always rose in the corner of my mouth
    and it still happens til this day
    but while i always heard my mother
    always knew my mother
    all throughout time
    i had to find you

and i found you as a very young man
    when our greatest feat of all
    was when we both finally said
    i love you.

Angels For Jasmine (A Letter)

dear sister,

do you know the angels that guard your bedside?
   do you know their names?
   you probably don't
   you don't enjoy favors
   until the last minute
   afraid that it may be stripped from you
   but i put those angels their myself
   trust
   my dear sister
   nothing will tear away those angels from you

you are protected
   you are known
   you exist to let God know
      that He has gotten at least one thing right about mankind

do you know you make Him laugh?
   do you know you challenge Him to Be A Better God?
   He appreciates it

ANGELS FOR JASMINE (A LETTER)

you are a sliver of light in my thinning darkness
   i have found part of my path
   and thanks to you
   the thick darkness does not cover my face

you are my best friend
   nothing could possibly heal me faster
   than hearing your laughter
   and nothing frightens me more
   not even God Himself
   than the mere thought of losing you

you are loved by me
   dear sister
   and you don't have to say it back
   i know you
   just keep hold of your more-than-deserved happiness
   and never lose your voice.

You've Got Mail

one week away from town
   and i returned
   only to one piece of mail

no love letter
   no stupid ad mail
   showing me furniture and food i don't need
   no,
   not even that

mail from a collections agency.

how did they find me?
   i moved!

Peace

i stand still,
   yet the waves still crash,
   and rumble,
   and yearn to touch the shore.

i stand still,
   and the world still spins,
   but it does not revolve around my stagnancy,
   nor would it revolve around me in motion.

i thought peace was a still thing,
   a stopped entity or feeling;
   uninterrupted waters.

but is peace not the breeze that kisses the leaves,
   is peace not the warmth from movement in the cold?
   is peace not the sound of something or someone i love,
   is peace not the feeling of my body on the water floating above?

is peace not the stroke of my pen pouring my spirit -
   inked
     onto paper that originated from some far off forest,

and that same peace being the breeze
that kissed the leaves
and the bark of the trees?

is peace not interconnected?
   is peace not a living thing?

if not, why do men of war suffer without it?
   if not, why do mothers of newborns that cry,
   yearn for the quiet,
   as does the child yearn for that of which it does not yet know by name,
   only touch,
   feeling,
   sound
   taste?

if peace is not a living thing flowing,
   woven by its own thread in nature,
   between the flesh of spirits contained,
   then why do i not find it when i am still at night, alone in the dark?
   far from movement except my own,
   far from sound except the ambience that creeps in
   and the soft thuds from my ear on soft pillows?

when i stop,
   my thoughts settle,
   like the aftermath of a storm.

puddles,
   flooded drains,

PEACE

    wet asphalt,
    broken branches,
    power outages,
    flames burnt out from candles burning all night,
    lost dogs.

and when i come out and collect the branches,
    when the sun starts to dry the waters,
    when the smoke breaks away from the wick,
    when the dogs find their way home-
      peace is waving.

Sky High Loves

the gold of the sun
   staring down like a yellow eye
   is up before me
   listening to my early morning rustling
   twisting
   turning
   yearning in bed

laughing at the numerous times i've snoozed my alarm

she hears my morning prayer i mutter
   eyes still closed
   but awake
   thanking God for another day
   and the day goes on until she sets

the shape of the moon
   full or starving
   surprises me with her presence
   as i always notice miss luna when she is just above the horizon
   and when my bank account is teetering just above negative

she watches me stumblin' into another bar
   spendin' my last few dollars for
   what i hope will turn out to be a great time

and when i get home
   ripping off all of my clothes
   'cept my favorite boxers
   whether i'm with a woman or alone

she bleeds through the blinds
   lingering upon my wall that would be shadows
   if not for her angelic presence

she hears my nightly prayers
   the last few songs i play before bed
   the movie or show in the background
   the rustling in my sheets as i rub my ankles
   and feet like crickets
   to get comfortable

and she stays with me until i am sleep
   she does not bother me as she leaves

BUT the sun blazes me awake
   "God almighty is it hot today!"

and i realize
   finally
   that the sun has missed me
   i am sorry for my ignorance
   miss ignis

forgive me

what a lucky man i am -
   two beautiful women in love with me!

No Name

now knowing
that i want to live
i will learn to love
just as God learned to love man

in time.

Words For A Sweet Lady

would you trust me to liberate you?
   oh, gentle lady
   there is nothing wrong with you

only all is wrong in the world
   and yet
   life insists balance because of you

the world beneath your feet
   as it should be
   you're worshiped by the flowers

the reeds
   the roots
   the beat of mother earth

the waves of the night
   pulled by the moon
   that keeps its shining light on you

it's nature
   as all things should be

WORDS FOR A SWEET LADY

to be in truth

to all be correct
   to be gentle
   to be surviving

to be in love
   yin and yang
   because of you
   ...
   yet, i am a man
   maybe it isn't my place
   to say you could or can

pack your bags
   or kick his ass out
   draw up another plan

but every woman
   in my life
   has worn similar shoes as you

i only ever
   truthfully wanted
   and still want what's best for you

i couldn't do the job
   an exes father couldn't
   back when he was alive

words to give

preparing a table for his daughter
but too soon did his end arrive

my mothers prayers
for all her three kids
sent up with projected fear

six sisters
her and all of them
follow grandma and mother dear

2020
protested a college assault
a crowd and my sister with me

fearful of the thought
the things possible
when she moved from the city

demanding prayers
God show your true strength
the least He could do for my sister

it's been four years
since she left the west
and everyday i miss her

a good friend
told an insecure man
she got back up

WORDS FOR A SWEET LADY

that she knows good men
   should he ever get the bright idea
   to try and act up

it's not all men
   it's not all bears
   but could that be naivety?

a tricky thing
   that God learned from
   we speak in 11 days

it could add up
   teeny little things
   like micro-aggressions

somethin' i talked about
   back in high school
   in therapy sessions

the line between us
   man and woman
   should never have sown such a divide

its patriarchy patterns
   you're always right
   its barely subtle lines

what can i do
   what actions can i take
   for you to safely shine?

subtext
   read between the lines
   guilty by association

speaking out
   with another commitment
   feminist appropriation?

humor found me
   in my darkest of moments
   a thing about coping

somewhere deep
   in the thick darkness
   is a heart hoping

there i go
   mansplaining again
   hope i don't provoke

but i pray you leave
   'cause even unintentionally
   he'll always be a bear to poke

i don't know how you feel
   can't even ask
   if you really love him

but i do know
   that you talk to God
   and His phone keeps buzzin'

WORDS FOR A SWEET LADY

...
 if i am not to be the one
 that liberates you
 from harms said and harms done

i pray
 you liberate yourself
 sweet lady

Dear Juliet

i am only resting
   bear with me
   in my slumber
   the poison was within me
   but i have spat out
   half of my bloody innards
   just to evict that falsehood
   and i will heal
   for the stage lights are off
   but i promise
   i am only resting
   even in the cover of darkness
   i can still see flickering
   the pale ghost light
   beaming upon my eyelids
   a mirage
   no, a path
   a statement
   that light will always
   pierce the veil
   of the abyss

DEAR JULIET

i am never truly lost
   unless i give you
   the last goodbye
   but i have turned away
   from wishes and prayers of death
   abrupt and committed
   i have freed those thoughts
   from the lowest chambers of my heart
   where i felt it so very deeply
   and i have found that
   i want life
   in preciousness and pitfalls
   in pleasure and pain

whether
   when i awake
   and you are still waiting for me
   or if i find myself
   in solitude
   i have committed myself
   to living.

Son

son
   when you gonna see the sun?
   when you gonna go on the run?
   chasing the things i've not seen
   chasing the things from my dreams

son
   whenever you find the one
   hold her as close as you can
   but be not the smothering hand
   just try the best that you can

son
   when you going back to God?
   don't ever call Him a fraud
   He's been plowing your path
   steered you away from the odds

son
   when it's my time to go
   when the wind is calling me home
   turn my body into dust

SON

    and i don't want people in rows

son
   i did the best that i could
   raising you three from a distance
   i did as a father should
   don't let me be misunderstood

I Hear You

i swing the door open to the diner
   table for two please
   they walk me to a booth
   i sit facing the door
   you never know

i haven't seen you in half a year
   you went to virginia with my sister
   shortly after that
   i fought my brother
   and today is thanksgiving

i keep staring at the door
   wondering how you look
   how you are
   it's only been half a year
   but it's been so long

my dad's always asking about you
   you always ask about him
   but y'all never talk directly
   only through your kids

I HEAR YOU

i keep staring at the door
   you haven't gotten here yet
   i'm worrying
   i shouldn't do that
   i know you're driving and almost here
   i'm just nervous

i hope you don't think
   that i blame you for everything
   it's been hard for all of us

i lost the car
   the house
   i shut a lot of people out
   even you for a time

a little over a year ago
   you suffered a heart attack
   and your daughter
   was your only child beside you

there was a time when
   my darkest of thoughts fled from me
   because i imagined, so vividly, the heartbreak
   it would have caused my dear sister
   and fear struck my heart
   like the stomping of Gods footsteps

i keep staring at the door
   is that you? no
   maybe this is you

yeah

baseball cap
    fleece jacket
    your black apron and dress shirt still on
    black tennis shoes at the brink of being worn out

my disheveled beard
    nappy hair and black shades
    big flannel jacket and hoodie to hide my added weight
    blue jeans and dirty sneakers

you look my way and i stand
    hugging you in my arms
    i wanted to hug a bit longer
    but you gave up quicker than usual
    i sit and feel a way about how much you talk
    but i listen anyway
    because you're my mother
    and because i finally noticed the wrinkles on your hands

i think about the time i told you
    that i was struggling more mentally
    feeling as though i was on the edge
    i never told you that i was on calls with suicide hotlines
    but you said that i should make a gratitude list
    reminding myself that i have something
    someone
    to be grateful for
    something
    and someone

I HEAR YOU

to remain alive for
even if it was one thing
even if it was one person

even it were simple things
things that disappeared from my sight
in the tunnel vision of mental trauma

to see another friend
to see another sunset
to hear a family members voice
to write another poem

to cook another meal
to watch another movie
to dance to another one of your eighties songs
to light and smell another candle

to just simply remain alive.

often times i found myself doubting my dreams
or putting my small wants above others bigger needs
and you've always been the one to try and mend things
a reason why shane and i began speaking again
the reason why i still take on acting today
the reason i still smile today
because you reminded me of the word *faith*.

i stared at that list of ten things
it gave me a lifeline
being as long as it needed to be

until life presented me with the next lifeline
or until i created the next one myself
i don't know if you know
how many times you unintentionally saved me

i think about another time
   when i taught myself how to play acoustic guitar
   and i wanted to show it off to you for your birthday
   some months before you and my stepdad at the time
   moved to oregon with shane
   allowing me and jasmine to live and bond together
   so i played a song and you recorded it
   i thought i had played a rendition
   of "mama you've been on my mind"
   because that's what i remembered practicing
   but when i found the video again some years ago
   turns out i settled for playing you
   a shitty version of "twist and shout"

i'd like to say i watched that eighties movie
   about a charismatic, teenage high school skipper
   the day before or day of playing that song
   but i didn't
   it's the only version i knew
   i didn't know of the brothers version
   until i became a wedding dj
   following in my dads footsteps

my memory takes me even further back
   eighteen years ago
   meade village circle

I HEAR YOU

    meade village road
    back when you would blast your music
    cleaning the house with the windows open
    on saturday or sunday mornings
    eggs, scrapple or sausage, pancakes
    God knows i had an unruly love for whole milk back then

and at night
    you'd sit me down
    well past bedtime
    at the kitchen table
    my siblings asleep or
    in their rooms upstairs

but me and you
    up late
    you'd have a drink

you tell me about a man
    a Man named Jesus
    in your hand
    a penny

you'd tell me He's the King of kings
    that He gave you all three of us
    by God's will

"this penny"
    you'd say
    "you and Jesus are the same
    the same bronze color as this penny

the Sons of God"
tell me that our hair -
wool-like -
is the same

you were the first to tell me
   that Jesus is not white
   that the Man we worship
   was not a white savior
   and at some point in my mind
   darkening overtime
   i may have forgotten that

you always gave me the sense
   to love myself
   but somehow along the way
   when the attacks were from within myself
   i lost that

you'd tell me about my birth
   how i was
   allegedly
   the easiest out of all three of us
   for you to push out

tell me how special i was
   what i meant to you
   how i was your brown sugar baby
   a nickname my closest friends rub in my face

tell me that my brother

I HEAR YOU

the warrior
my sister
the princess
i was…
i can't remember

i just know
   that i love you
   and if i don't say it enough
   i hope your memory of me tells you
   no matter how much we drift apart

and i hope that it also tells you
   that i've always listened to you
   no matter how you talked
   with tears
   with laughter
   with calmness
   with anger
   with the other version of you
   when your inebriated eyes glistened
   or with the hope and conviction
   of believing i was someone worthy of living
   just for the simple fact
   of me being your son

i've always listened
   because
   i've always
   heard
   you.

Letter To Shane

dear brother,

whoever told you the world hated you
   they lied

i had to break away from you
   to become my own man

you could never see it
   but i looked up to you
   idolized you
   praised you
   and a part of that came out of me
   the day we reconciled
   a week or two
   before we fought each other

you said you were the example
   for me to not follow
   that all of your mistakes
   was something for me to avoid

LETTER TO SHANE

but you said it
   as if you wanted to keep living your life that way
   with no adjustment
   no victory
   as if that was it
   as if that was all you had

i yelled
   "i don't want you to keep making mistakes!"
   and you said you saw a fire in me
   for the first time
   but what you didn't know
   was that it was a yearning for your perfection
   was that the fire was love and passion
   the frustration of what seemed to me your inaction
   in real life and in my distant night

how many dreams i couldn't save you in
   how many prayers seemed to fall on Closed Ears
   how many nights
   as a kid
   i would watch you sleeping
   to see
   if you were still breathing

maybe it wasn't fair
   in all my life 'til this point
   to hold you to such standards of perfection
   but how could i not?
   i am your keeper

and we confronted each other
   over the fact that
   at one point or another
   we both tried taking our lives
   and over our indifferences

we released so much rage on each other
   balled up over time

the different choices we made
   the ones we made together

would you have respected me
   if i just took it on the chin
   and didn't fight back?
   no
   and i wouldn't have respected myself either

and yet
   i am sorry
   for all of it
   ...
   maybe i should have walked
   into a facility with you
   despite the fact that you threatened
   to fight me if i got out of the car
   our mom crying behind the wheel

but i couldn't see you were afraid
   all i saw was your temper and pride
   something i'd seen for so long

LETTER TO SHANE

    that i mistook it for who you were

what would my help have been anyways?
    i question myself in that regard
    was it truly for helping you or unburdening myself?
    unfortunately, maybe both things are true
    ...
    i will remember our prayer
    a week before we fought
    as our true brotherhood
    the only time
    we ever
    truly
    embraced each other

not the playing around as kids
    or showing each other things we enjoyed
    not the birthdays
    not the games we played
    not the times
    when you'd bust out a rhyme
    not when
    you'd tell me to stay up late and
    keep the door unlocked
    'cause you were goin' to see your girlfriend
    or the times when
    you'd lecture me
    or just ramble
    chase your dog together
    or she'd chase us
    not even the time when

you saved our mother
from seeing the end

in all of those moments
we had already knew that we were brothers

but that entire day
where we talked about the wolf
the things you'd felt and seen
in the facilities you've been in
the things you held yourself back from
the misunderstandings from our loved ones
the real nightmares you shed a light on
we put our souls on display
for each other

words
not cryptic messages
or subtext
to decipher or explain

that prayer
will always be my love letter to you
for your heart knows what i said
when i held your hands
and spoke to God

through all the pain
unsaid words
involuntary disdain

LETTER TO SHANE

you ring true
   as my blood
   my brother
   one of the starting pieces
   of my soul
   that i was placed on this earth with

as the younger brother
   you never let me be in your shadow
   you always tried to put me right beside you
   even when you couldn't put right before wrong

but no matter the angst
   no matter the ache in my heart
   i will always keep you there
   in my breast
   in my chest
   in my soul
   for as long as day isn't night

find your path, dear brother,
   to rehabilitation
   to the pursuit of happiness and healing
   i love you
   i pray you find your victory
   i pray that you will forgive me
   i pray you will forgive yourself, too.

i keep hope alive
   for i know that if i can bury the lion
   i know you can bury the wolf

and on that day, we will laugh together again.

Your Uncle's Words

where do i begin?
   mom and him
   and your mom
   they say you look like him
   hopefully he'll be there for your first steps
   for your first dress
   for your first spin

maybe you'll make him allow himself a new start
   maybe you'll make him walk a better path
   one that doesn't lead him in the dark
   you're a light inna complex life
   a need for survival - water for noah's ark
   that's just blessed math
   make him want to hold love more
   and let go of wrath

there's a lot more love in him than in this book
   that's for sure
   i mean look at you
   what he'd do for you
   to let you know you're pure

of his baggage
    he won't let you see it loom
    he'll heal and get rid of it just for you
    all the trials taught him to manage
    in his heart – there's a special room
    a new pink crib
    a dog named shiara
    he'll keep you safe there after he's done tidying up with a broom

Kinder Man

what kind of man do you want to be?
  a kinda man?
  a kind man

too many tough men
  too many rough men
  too many how much men
  too many lost touch men

weak men
  freak men
  improper men
  show stopper men

idolized men
  desensitized men
  unGodly men
  do-wrongly men

i'd rather be a kinder man
  kindness can snip the tether of trauma
  if you'd only try it, man

learned to tell my homies
   i love 'em

learned to tell my cousin
   i love him

learned to tell my brother
   i love him

use the word
   before it's too late, man.

What's Your Name?

some love to tell the black man what he shouldn't feel
   some love to tell him that he'll never heal
   some love to see the black man start
   some love to see him keep hate in his heart

from a baby boy – asphalt burns and ashy knees
   to finding the man within myself in my twenties being pressed by the police
   and the world trying to make a baby think his skin inferior
   to bring about his question "would God accompany me?"

made me want to ask God to tell my grandmother
   her daughter's generosity rubbed off on me
   and in the same breath
   tell Him her pain is never lost on me

no matter how strong the flower
   the roots hurt as they search the soil to truly plant themselves
   and they grow
   thankful – the rain softens the earth
   maybe one day to feed another with the hurt

SOULPUNK

we learn to remain
    with stories that are birthed out of love and pain
    the bonds and laughs we gain
    out of shared strength and shame
    and the momentum to keep playing the game
    reminds me of every black mans name

All That I Carry

*i have made it out of the dungeon
and as i behold the mirror
i see the truth for what it is
human
as i am*

*sinner and saint
the battle between love and lie
a soul made quaint
with no time to die*

Remain

in my dreams of wonder
    of pain intent on bringing raging waters to my eyes
    joy like a fine smile on a lovers face
    churches that i've found and left
    and the inbetweens

i awake
    remembering who you are
    and why i am awake

alas
    i have found him
    i've known the fucker for so long
    i am him
    i am the man in the mirror
    and i have found my home

a desire inside my own heart
    to keep going
    the misty cloud does not hinder me

she still doesn't yell about the things that i do

REMAIN

i've come to understand we're much different – her and i
even though she is my blood
even though i am her son
even so, we are different

i laid, unmoved by you, for years
   but i am free from the depths
   of waiting for your love
   forever my days were lived
   on yearner's eve
   yet, i find myself free
   as are my dreams, from the sandman
   facing the discomfort of loneliness
   and in doing so
   i've discovered self love in solitude
   something that may have escaped me all my life
   had i kept yearning for you

i remember you
   you were my mothers brother
   my brothers favorite uncle
   you passed early in my life
   too soon in yours
   i can't remember your voice
   but i remember where it came from
   and i remember sitting on your bed
   days after your funeral
   thinking of you
   scared because the door somehow locked on its own
   that week i learned of real life
   as i watched my mother cry

delivering a speech over your casket
interrupted by tears
and i learned of death
from your absence
and what it did to them
abruptly – without preparations
or
a proper chance at goodbye
a word that can change the trajectory
of one's life

your memory reminds me
    the air on earth is rich with hope and chance
    but the time is short so we must make it sweet

that same time has given me the present and clarity
    and so i walk in light
    of knowing myself
    and loving myself
    through oblivion

i am what remains from the passing of the mist
    of the thick darkness that covered my face
    and i am no longer surrounded.

You Snuck Into God's Office?

yeah
   He was doing something
   i heard
   beeping noises – typing, too
   in intervals
   sporadically
   like computer systems from the eighties
   He was working on something

"on what?"

one... BEEP... two... BEEP BEEP...
   run that back, J.C.
   one... BEEP... two... BEEP BEEP...
   no, let's try another...

i don't know
   "could you see?"

no, it was dark
   but He was there
   studious like a scientist

testing something

"did He see you?"

three... BEEP BEEP BEEP...
   no, too much
   maybe we'll go longer?
   shorter?
   okay, try it
   one.. BEEP.. two.. BEEP BEEP..
   maybe
   yeah, that's looking like the right direction
   hey, you comin' or goin'?

yeah, He did
   i don't know how
   i mean
   it was dark
   i get it
   He's God
   trust me, CORNY, i get it
   but how'd He see me
   surrounded by darkness
   and working
   at the same time?

We ain't got all day
   J.C. to H.S.
   H.S. copy
   show 'em the ropes
   slowly please

YOU SNUCK INTO GOD'S OFFICE?

see if they [REDACTED]
copy

"that's intense
so what happened next?"

The Man Upstairs

"took you long enough"
   took me? what about You? how many years?
   "ah... too many, I know... Way too many.
   but that is why you're here, do you understand?"
   no... my entire life i've spent running,
   running in spirals to no gain.
   "you were always running towards Something...
   walk with Me"

i follow Him up a set of stairs
   into a warm and spacious sunlit room.
   He gets me a black coffee.
   He gets the same thing for Himself.
   we grab a seat by a small window
   the sunlight gently radiates on both of us.
   yet, i can't help but notice an office swivel chair
   across the room
   facing a different window
   a mere omniscient pane
   where the sun brightly beams in.

"sean, i must tell you something."

THE MAN UPSTAIRS

yes?

"in order for you to take this in,
   I need you to be a student —
   even after our time here.
   you must remain forever learning
   forever yearning for correct knowledge
   performing corrective actions
   and finding comprehension of many things.
   understand that praying for it
   opens the door of trials."

i understand—

"do you?
   I have placed you in front of many doors
   I have even opened some of them for you.
   all I ever needed was for you to walk through,
   but cowardice has caused your hesitations
   just as much as jealousy and the want of a different life
   has caused some of your anger and despair.
   you have been lacking in humility and restraint,
   and thus,
   the studies and lessons trickle upon you,
   when I need it to be wired into your blood,
   so that you do not commit the same mistakes
   but that you apply what you have learned throughout time
   to live a dignified life of wisdom, not doomed repetition.
   I did not put you here for stagnancy."

then i will seek to understand.

"promise."

what?

"shall I waste another word or will it click?
   I cannot take your nonchalant approach to seeking
   when you have been passive to conflict for far too long,
   and that is precisely what I Am presenting to you.
   how can I expect you to confront yourself
   if you cannot even confront trespasses against you?"

You've been the biggest trespass against me.

"Me? by what rules?"

by Your own!
   You abandoned me.

"I've given you community—"

no, not them.
   not my family, my friends
   or the arts community—
   You. YOU abandoned me.

"**YOU STOPPED LOOKING UP.**
   ...
   something your brother reminded you to do
   when you were both children.
   that hour has passed — you are a man
   and you still tilt your crown to woes and self pity.

THE MAN UPSTAIRS

    Am I responsible for all your successes and failures?
    must I bear the balance by Myself,
    or will you finally take responsibility
    in the matter of your own life?
    a life which you've actively denounced."

i burst to my feet
    rushing away from Him and glaring out the omniscient window
    holding back the water works
    and as the sunlight clashes with my face
    i catch the faintest glimpse
    of my reflection in the pane

"My son... if you live in avoidance
    out of fear
    you will never be resolute.
    ...
    I Am not asking you to seek to understand
    I Am telling you I need your promise for transformation
    which requires you to be open.
    this will not be an easy conversation,
    so I need you to be honest and raw — here and now."

i turn back to Him
    after the new found air has kissed my lungs
    and i join Him back at the table

okay... i promise to be open.

"good.
    ...

in the beginning, every time I turned My head, something happened.
when Eve bit into the fruit, I wasn't looking.
when cain killed abel, I wasn't looking.
these two incidents have infused a sort of cycle,
or rhythm (if you will),
into the very laws of your world.
whether I Am looking or not anymore.
it is as if a child is playing peek-a-boo with their parent
they will keep playing
whether the parent is looking or not.
do you understand? "

no

"the imperfections and mistakes of the first humans to walk the earth
is the causality for everything that followed.
temptation, oath-breaking, greed, jealousy, murder…
the five things that damned humanity.
the sixth? naivety.
but on the flip side of that,
are the six things that can redeem humanity
which are—"

why did You allow for so many things since then?
the punishments?

"perhaps it is My eye.
you take time moment to moment – by the very second.
I, on the other hand, see it altogether
as it unfolds and in its entirety.
I stretched My hands and needed to stretch My Sons just to save it

all.
   free will is the master mankind,
   I am just a whistle in the wind.
   a revelation in a hurricane
   to save, distract, guide
   pull in, push away, search for…
   the very first person I ever failed was Eve.
   I should have warned Her there was someone else in the Garden
   that She should be aware of.
   but if a parent does not punish or teach their child in some way,
   they will become combative to any form of resistance down the road.
   I decided to set that punishment at the very beginning for everyone.
   low and behold, that failure resulted in the third incident."

what's the third incident?

"the world failing women.
   as a result of My naivety
   it has infused itself into the very fabric of the world.
   women are the heartbeat of the planet.
   the very reason for mankind's existence after the Garden…
   there were multiple times in My planning
   when I wanted to send the ultimate plague and end your people's suffering
   in maybe the most peaceful way."

peaceful?

"hmph, believe Me, I hear Myself.
   women alone could end mankind.

after all, looking back, there are some things I'm sure even you would say
    makes the world seem irredeemable...
    but My Son talked me out of it."

what was it going to be?

"mass infertility"

I need another fucking coffee... can He hear this?
    if so... forgive me for swearing—

"still your thoughts, My son, I Am speaking.
    ...because He went down and made His sacrifice,
    He can see moment to moment,
    second to second – like you.
    like mankind.
    He told me to remember that humans are not perfect,
    therefore humans can and must heal.
    to remember the joys of a child.
    remember the sound of their laughter echoing throughout
    the pains and horrors of the world.
    and to remember those who hoped for that child for as long as they could.
    whether they were in that child's life entirely
    until they perished
    or if they were only there in the mere moment
    of the child's birth.
    they had hoped something would work out."

why can't you trade the horrors of mankind for peace?

THE MAN UPSTAIRS

"if I show and tell everything,
   you'll miss the discovery.
   and that is where peace is.
   it isn't still in perfection,
   it is in the gathering of pieces
   of tranquility."

then give us that!
   give us that comfort, that peace!
   give us those pieces without us having to fight for it.
   God, you have left me so conflicted,
   i've been holding on for so long,
   just for my loved ones at times it feels like.
   do You know how long i wanted to just get it over with?
   to just end it all??
   but i didn't,
   and i still will not
   because i see my younger self
   my future
   i see my friends
   and i see my loved ones
   other people...
   and...
   they need to know it's okay to cry.
   they need to know it's going to be okay.
   that laughter, love and serenity will find them again.
   that there is something greater on the other side of the pain.
   i can't bear to show my weakness around them -
   around anyone,
   but sometimes it slips through.
   all this pressure i've built up inside and i have to take it all

one moment at a time.
one awful mistake,
one moment of cowardice,
one gone grandmother,
one woman i could not get rid of my suicidal thoughts for to appreciate,
all – everything – one moment at a time,
but i have become too scatter brained
replaying all the moments in my mind
until that's all i hear in my head.

all my grief and defeats,
my woes and anxieties
bouncing around until they are caught
all in one cohesive moment,
one burdened stream.

i could not save my family from harm.
i could not save myself.
i could not fix these problems.
i cannot comfort them enough…
and You cannot give me comfort.

"you cannot grow in comfort, My dear boy."

but —

"what greater comfort could I give,
other than My love…
to bring you here…
and to say that I Am sorry?

THE MAN UPSTAIRS

   ...
   your sympathies are not weaknesses.
   you used to not be so pitifully driven,
   yet you were empathetic and responsive —
   no matter the weight."

i have grown weary of such things, Father.
   that is why i beg of you
   please
   just give me peace

"where is your courage?
   your ambition? your momentum?
   you ask as if it is some materialistic thing.
   even if I *gave* you peace
   you would find some way to disrupt it
   for man is often his own agent of chaos."

at least let me figure out if that'd be true or not—

"you have helped drive three friends
   including yourself
   away from suicide.
   do you still not understand?"

no

"you've been given the answer earlier.
   you ask what the suffering is for
   maybe it is so the word *save* can exist
   what if you are here to save one another

everyday
see how long you can save each other?"

we wouldn't need saving if —

"can you not hear the clouds?"

what? hear what from the clouds?

"you can't hear the clouds yet...
   what if I told you I was writing another Book?"

i'd say great
   because i want my own Word,
   not the Word that's been tainted and abused for thousands of years.

"what is the difference between the truth of My Word
   whether it was or is used for good or not?
   those people will be dealt with – My Word still rings true"

but You can see how it's hard to justify Your Word and You
   when It's been used to claim land, blood, power, and countless livelihoods

"but It has also been used to combat those very same atrocities...
   free will taunts man in good or bad nature.
   I've threaded hundreds of needles in every man's individual life.
   it is up to mankind to figure out which ones he tightens
   and which ones he bites off in his dog-like nature...
   why must you be selfish in wanting a Word of your own?"

THE MAN UPSTAIRS

because we are a part of the same dog.
    in the honorable church, it is the same teeth as the corrupt one.
    i'm exhausted of sharing the same Word
    with oppressors, white supremacists, sexual abusers, bad actors,
    inhuman priests and pastors, abusive parents or partners, grifters -
    You name it.

"exhausted
    and yet, you yourself are not sinless.
    nor have you even finished the entire book"

hey—

"you must take accountability for how long you've allowed part of your soul
    to be filled with gloom and pride in not reading the Word you call *tainted*"

HEY—

"if you want another cup, just ask."

… sure.

He grabs me another cup of black coffee.

"besides, you love the book of jonah"

well… true…

"and he had trouble stewarding things I gave him,

much like yourself"

b-but in Your Word's entirety, the bad apples that follow You
seem to me
that they outweigh the good.
and so i think It's too tainted.

"when did you become the watchdog of man under my Word,
as if there is no accumulation of small acts of goodness?
and in the same breath, such an ungrateful,
selfish,
grandiose narcissist
with the audacity to demand your own Word?"

i...
i don't know.

i tell Him... shamefully.

i don't know...

"now you know nothing?
...
good.
...
if I were to give you a machete -
sharpened and perfectly made to fit in the hand of every human,
would you use it to provide, protect and preach?"

why does it have to be a weapon?

THE MAN UPSTAIRS

"you called the machete a weapon
   because you and mankind liken My Word to such descriptions.
   you hold onto it from the hilt
   but you should be holding it close to protect you and others
   and only change your stance so as to provide or preach
   a show of strength, integrity and grit
   akin to the rod and staff.
   a tool, not a weapon."

but a weapon should be used in all its created intent

"it need not. I tell you, yet again, My son,
   it is not a weapon, but it is a tool.
   it could destroy, but it needn't do that"

unless?

"unless? there is no unless.
   My Word is truth, salvation and justice,
   it is never for preaching or justifying obliteration.
   reigns and kingdoms may fall,
   armies and wicked ways may crumble,
   wolves in sheep's clothing may be revealed and defeated,
   but it is all so that light replaces the dark,
   so that evil is replaced with good.
   My Word's intent is to shine a light on darkness,
   to save,
   not inhumanely destroy or subjugate."

that's a very fine line to toe…
   i mean, You know It's used that way, right?

don't You ultimately decide that?
are the same Hands that created us
not the same Ones that drew mankind to create the atomic bomb?

"man and his curious cat
   wanted a gift from prometheus;
   I am far from it"

so mankind's curiosity is the cop out?

"must I slap you over the head?
   show Me your smart mouth again.
   free will, My naive son, free will.
   must you inherit such an old trait from Me?
   how long must you play the role of a fool?
   you dropped out of college and I still fed you.
   have I not given you enough to grow intellectually?"

no, actually i don't believe You have—

suddenly, He is standing.
   i'm not even sure if i saw Him get up—

"do you want to wrestle?"

is...
   is that a joke?

"what?"

are you mocking me?

THE MAN UPSTAIRS

    about 8th grade when i was gonna join
    the wrestling team in kentucky?

"no, I would never joke about that"

oh, okay. it just seemed like
    You thought maybe i wasn't gonna join anyways—

"you saw them practicing headlocks,
    you've always been claustrophobic
    it made sense for you to not join after that."

alright, no need to be specific.

"were you always this insecure?"

excuse me?

"how did you jump to such a conclusion?
    what if I was talking about your college play?"

i mean… were You?

"no, I am being as serious as possible.
    do you want to wrestle?"

You think i want a dislocated hip??
    i'm already 26 with a bad back

"then wise up
    and be quiet for a moment."

okay.

"oh, you listen well don't you?"

sorry..?

"**greed** grows like a tree
   in the hearts of man —
   the master of many deceitful traits —
   so you must repeatedly nip it at the buds.
   for if a greedy man finds out he can take a step,
   he will take a ruler.
   if he finds out he can take a ruler,
   he will take your name.
   if he finds out he can take your name,
   he will take your home.
   if he finds out he can take your home,
   he will demonize you and take your land.
   if he finds out his demonization of you allows him to be righteous in the eyes of most men,
   he will bury the truth with something least likely to be successfully challenged,
   or dug up (if you will)"

how can i hear the things He says in parentheses?

and what's that?

"Me.
   that I made man do it.
   that it was written by the Author of authors.

THE MAN UPSTAIRS

    I Am mankind's scapegoat of all greater goods and greater evils; forever questioned if I Am looking or not."

peekaboo…

"precisely.
    …
    you want your own Word?"

yes.

"not until you've figured out the one I already gave you."

what's that?

"Forgiveness."

i am sorry, Father, but i do not have much room left in my heart.

"not in your heart.
    your heart is doing better these days,
    but no, not there.

in your soul."

…
    all i can say is that i will try.

"that is good enough for Me."

i just have one more question…

what happens after all this?

"after what?"

life.

"you don't think that is in the discovery
   of your journey?"

i don't know what to think.

"I've told you before,
   whispered the truth to you when you were in the womb,
   but you wouldn't remember.
   no one ever does.
   and if I told you again,
   you would curse Me for giving you a spoiler."

you're joking about the afterlife?
   You WERE making fun of me earlier,
   about the wrestling team!

"the sarcasm escaped you for once
   but please, spare me your hypocrisy,
   laughter has gotten you through the darkest of times.
   and when the child plays peekaboo by themselves
   they are still laughing.
   besides,
   there are more important things to consider."

what's more important than the afterlife?

THE MAN UPSTAIRS

"the most important thing is
   and has always been
   love,
   which includes you living now,
   dear boy,
   and… understanding
   that you were right, to some degree,
   about a *tainting*.
   though, I would not use such a word,
   rather,
   My Word has undergone *alterations* —
   ones I do not approve of."

how many?

"enough to get the world
   where it is today."

don't You have control over this?
   why isn't it just as simple as an override?

"shall I be your master?
   or shall I let you be?
   …
   now
   you wanted answers
   this is the weight of having such demands.
   I've met you where you are,
   and where you have been countless times,
   but you will never meet Me Where I Am—
   that is the distance between us.

there will always be a gap,
    you are better off trying not to close such a thing
    for your mind would crumble in My sandals.
    ...
yet, I will tell you again
to remain a student, My son.
you will find
there is much to gain
when approaching from nothingness
for there, you will find yourself
there, you will find My many truths
Ones that may become singers."

Soulpunk

"how do you live?"

i live for a chance to love
   but i'd have to dare to suffer
   to have that truth.

what better risk could there be
   for one to take
   other than to see
   feel
   give or be given
   create or find
   that which is divine?
   that which is the true enduring language of humanity?

love itself -
   as it encompasses a multitude of things
   the one true thing i know
   that can resurrect and restore the soul.

here, now, amongst the living
   i have learned of fate

and i can no longer sustain soaring under
i must take the wings of life and make them my own.

for when my heart is beaten
    battered
    exhausted
    ripped apart and healed
    all to be ripped apart
    and healed again
    as are the ebbs and flows of humanity —

i am reminded
    that my soul is the chamber in which my heart resides
    it is a living soul
    obtaining everything that i am
    everything i once was
    everything i will become
    and i must nurture it.

the soul is an immortal thing
    and so i leave proof of it here
    flaws and all
    whether it resides partially on these pages,
    or in the heavens,
    in the future
    where i hope it does

i sleep tonight
    praying to live another day on earth
    to get it right

because life must go on.

About the Author

Hopefully this has shown at least one of you that you are not alone in your struggles and to do as I should have done sooner - if you are drowning, reach out. You never know who will take your hand. Professionals, services, friends, family, teachers, communities, tribes, hotlines - there is something or someone out there.

Please rate and leave a review where you've purchased your copy. Be sure to follow me on social media. Don't be a stranger! Thank you for reading.
   - Wade P.

Instagram @wade.s_p
   Bluesky @wxde.bsky.social
   Substack @cowboyyojimbo